P9-CEG-590

Beyond Me

Grounding Youth Ministry in God's Story

Wendell J. Loewen

Faith & Life Resources
A division of Mennonite Publishing Network
Mennonite Church USA and
Mennonite Church Canada

Scottdale, Pennsylvania
Waterloo, Ontario

Library of Congress Cataloging-in-Publication Data
Loewen, Wendell J., 1964–
  Beyond me: grounding youth ministry in God's story/Wendell J. Loewen.
    p. cm.
  Includes bibliographical references.
  ISBN 978-0-8361-9403-6 (pbk. : alk. paper)
  1. Church work with youth—Mennonites. I. Title.
  BV4447.L54 2008
  259'.23--dc22
                                        2008006559

    Unless otherwise noted, Scripture text is quoted, with permission,
from the New Revised Standard Version, ©1989, Division of Christian
Education of the National Council of Churches of Christ in the United
States of America.
Library of Congress Catalog Card Number: 2008006559
International Standard Book Number: 978-0-8361-9403-6
Design by Merrill R. Miller
Cover Photo: DesignPics/Con Tanasiuk
Printed in USA

Orders and information:
USA: 800-245-7894
Canada: 800-631-6535
www.mpn.net

Contents

Foreword

The average congregation is constantly tempted to ghettoize its youth ministry—to hire a young, energetic, guitar-playing Lone Ranger just out of college or seminary with two six shooters full of program ideas, charisma, and creativity. This individual is expected to create an entertaining program on the home range, and then go out into the frontiers of youth culture and "round up them youth and bring them in."

While a shift in thinking within youth ministry has taken place, this model continues to shape some congregational expectations today. Church leaders are quick to abdicate responsibility for ministry to and with their youth when a youth pastor is hired. There remains an unconscious desire to assign this ministry to a professional and to carry on with other priorities.

Such an approach may have worked in the past when social systems and institutions were less fragmented and when age groups were less segregated, but it's hardly the formula for the present. Teens are stressed, involved in sports, music lessons, part-time jobs; and feel pressure to excel at school. When you add spending time on the Internet, staying in touch with friends on Facebook, watching television, and listening to music, there is little time and space for solitude and less time for meaningful family interactions or church involvements.

Postmodern culture brings fragmentation that results in a crisis of identity and a lack of rootedness among teens. This sub-population is powerfully influenced by the media and is vulnerable to accepting its messages and values. According to Wendell Loewen, the most destructive weapon of our culture is the salvation story of consumption, creating consumers out of teens. Entertainment conglomerates and communications giants have joined forces to instill in our teens the desire to consume. This leads many adolescents to believe that their identity, belonging, and personal worth come through consumption. They are what they have, how much they have, and how quickly they can get it. Belonging is found in the brand and its community, and autonomy emerges from their power to spend in a way that brokers style and image.

In response, Wendell seeks to ground youth ministry in a kingdom-of-God theology. He believes that in the face of cultural influences, we can offer adolescents a contrasting story, the biblical narrative, upon which to build their lives. This counternarrative of God's reign has the potential to rescript the consumer culture's idea of "the good life," help youth gain their true sense of identity and fulfillment in Christ, and offer a sense of belonging in authentic community. Autonomy in this scenario means joining what God is already doing in the world and partnering with God to restore it to God's original intentions.

For youth pastors and other youth leaders, this means reorienting one's vision of ministry. First and foremost, it means seeing congregational youth ministry as *God's* ministry. When ministry is seen as God's ministry, it requires a stance of listening and observing what God is already doing in the lives of teens and in their world. God is present and active in the lives of adolescents and a first step in ministry includes assisting youth in noticing and naming this reality.

Second, it requires a commitment to making the youth and young adult ministry the work of the entire congregation. If separation and isolation are part of the problem, then integration and inclusion are part of the solution. Everything the church does teaches youth about the Christian faith: how to worship, how to treat each other, how to resolve conflict, how to pray, how to work together, how to share faith, how to live out faith. The impact can be maximized when intergenerational connections in the church are strong. The influence of one or two adults is not sufficient in a culture where youth are generally isolated from mature Christian adults and media messages dominate. More than ever, it takes a village, an entire church community, to pass on the faith to the next generation.

Third, youth have a lot to contribute to the body of Christ and to a hurting world. They do not need to wait until they have reached the age of eighteen or twenty-one to make a difference. A kingdom-of-God theology recognizes that persons of all ages can be prompted by the Spirit to live out kingdom values and respond to needs around them in life-giving ways.

Wendell Loewen has been a student of culture for many years and understands the adolescent journey. He offers a theological perspective that not only invites youth to a life of discipleship through and with the faith community, but also accompanies them as they live out kingdom values in a world of great need.

While Wendell offers many practical suggestions and illustrates this kingdom-driven approach through stories, he is not promoting a new model of ministry, nor does he present the magic bullet that will bring instant success with minimal effort. Rather, *Beyond Me* will help people in youth leadership to reflect more deeply on the purpose of ministry. It raises questions that can assist any youth leader in creating a ministry that is God-centered and holistic, attending to all the deeper needs of the adolescent.

This is the fourth book on youth ministry to be published by the Mennonite Church over the past twenty-one years. In 1987, Lavon Welty authored *Blueprint for Congregational Youth Ministry*. Though the culture was different from the present, this book challenged congregations to integrate their youth ministry into the life of the congregation and to coordinate all youth ministry efforts through a team ministry. Then in 1996, Mike Bogard provided a practical resource, *41 Ways to Build a Better Youth Group*, to assist congregations in enriching the worship, community life, service, and leadership development in their ministry to youth. In 2001, Carol Duerksen continued to push for a holistic approach in *Building Together: Developing Your Blueprint for Congregational Youth Ministry*. Building on Welty's book, it has provided further handles on how to implement such a ministry.

Wendell Loewen continues this conversation by reflecting on youth ministry in a postmodern era, especially as he recognizes the impact of consumerism and technology in the lives of teens. His theology of ministry addresses the issues of culture and adolescent development and helps the reader ground ministry in a theology of God's reign, which is beyond our own human constructs and depends on God's spirit.

If you want to work at aligning your ministry more closely with what God is doing in our world, this book will assist you. If you wish to be thoughtful about what you do in ministry, you have an excellent resource. *Beyond Me* invites you to plan and lead a ministry that will sustain youth in the long term, that strives to integrate them into the congregation and deepen their walk with God. This approach expects that youth leaders will be growing in their own discipleship as they accompany youth. It also envisions that youth will be invited into a community of faith where they will be encouraged by a community of adults, learning together what it means to follow Jesus in daily life.

Abe Bergen
Assistant Professor of Practical Theology
Canadian Mennonite University
December 2007

Preface

This book is a pen and paper stop on a long journey. For more than a dozen years I've been wrestling with ways to relate my Anabaptist-Mennonite and evangelical theology to current shifts in both culture and youth ministry. Along the way I've developed a growing belief that Anabaptism offers a compelling theology for our time.

Years ago I hosted a group of Mennonite Brethren pastors in our church. During one of our conversations, we lamented our denominational struggles. Someone floated the old idea that we should become less distinctive theologically and more generically Christian. That person assumed that such a shift would somehow generate growth in our churches. But one of the leaders, an urban pastor, rose to his feet and pled passionately with us. "We have something that our world is looking for," he implored. Specifically, he stressed our understandings of community and discipleship in following Jesus. He believed that our theological emphases addressed many of our contemporary cultural longings.

I'd grown up as a part of the General Conference Mennonite and Mennonite Brethren streams of the Anabaptist world, and I had always been a little bit bashful about what I knew of our distinctiveness. But here was someone boldly arguing for its significance and its potential. That day I began to embrace my Anabaptist theology.

As I started teaching youth ministry at Tabor College, I felt drawn to the biblical paradigm of God's reign as the heart of God's sweeping story in Scripture. For me, the image of God's kingdom captured the essence of God's people as a contrast community within the world. God's reign was a tangible framework for fleshing out our missional calling as agents of God's blessing to the world.

In the fall of 2001 I began my Doctor of Ministry studies at Fuller Theological Seminary in Youth and Family Ministries. During those four years, my eyes were opened to see teens and youth culture in new and unsettling ways. I came to realize that I didn't really know the teens to whom I'd been ministering. I was teaching prospective youth leaders about adolescents that no longer existed. I became acutely aware of the adolescent narrative and their need for ongoing, lifelong discipleship and authentic community—the very things that my Anabaptist theological heritage valued.

This book is my attempt to address the contours of the contemporary adolescent story as it relates to the counternarrative of God's reign. Even though I draw from the reflections of others on these two narratives, I am trying to achieve something that is rarely done in this field: bringing together in one discussion youth culture, adolescent development, theology, and youth ministry.

Beyond Me is not intended to address all the nuances of the issues it raises. For you, it may raise more questions than it answers. But that's where your engagement is important. Your voice, your perspectives, and your gifts are needed more than ever. Assuming you share my passion about doing youth ministry effectively while being faithful to the gospel, I hope these pages contribute to ongoing conversation. This book is not meant to be a final word on the subject, and it probably won't be my last word either.

I would like to acknowledge the contributions many people have made to this project. To my colleagues David Faber, Doug Miller, Lynn Jost, and Del Gray: your biblical and theological scholarship has propelled me on this journey. To my advisor at Fuller, Chap Clark: thank you for helping me see the needs of our teens today, and in the process rekindling my love for them.

To Ritch Hochstetler, thank you for casting the vision behind this book. Our collaboration on the "Thirsty for the Reign" articles for *Direction* in 2002 turned out to be the first step of an inspiring venture.

To the readers of my initial manuscript—Rick Bartlett, Abe Bergen, Andrew Brubacher Kaethler, Anna Rehan, Merv Stoltzfus, Kathy Weaver Wenger, and Bob Yoder: thank you so much for sharing your wisdom and insight. You challenged my thinking and sharpened my rhetoric. This is a better book because of your investment and time.

To Aleen Ratzlaff: your input in preparing the final manuscript was invaluable.

To Byron Rempel-Burkholder of Faith & Life Resources: without your keen editing and tireless work there would be no book. You are a true partner in this venture.

To Taylor, Peyton, and Preston: thanks for putting up with a distracted and often busy dad. But above all, to my spouse Shelly: thank you for taking this long journey with me, for your patience in reading the manuscript, and for keeping me grounded along the way.

Wendell J. Loewen
Hillsboro, Kansas

Introduction

"Does it Work?" Is Not Enough
A New Focus for Contemporary Youth Ministry

The teens are gone and the sounds of Shaun's coffee house have long faded. Shaun is confused. He doesn't think his youth outreach events work anymore. He picks up the evening's trash and mutters, "There were a lot of teens here, but where were their friends? They didn't come. They never do." For weeks Shaun encouraged his students to bring their unchurched friends to the coffee house. Instead, it was crowded with youth group regulars. Packing away the cappuccino machine, Shaun finally admits, "The bring-your-friends strategy hasn't worked for a long time."[1]

Shaun is wrestling with an emerging adolescent culture. Like many youth workers, he now recognizes that things are not as they used to be. But the shift has been difficult to identify. Could it be that the morphing face of adolescent culture requires quantum changes in youth ministry?

Reyna has also noticed some dramatic changes in her youth ministry in recent years. But her story is different. Reyna is a veteran volunteer youth leader of a small youth group. She's been ministering in a bedroom community just forty minutes from the city. Her church has no youth pastor. There are no other adult volunteers—just Reyna and about twenty teens.

For a long time, the signature trait of Reyna's ministry was her authentic relationships with students. There were no flashy programs, no hot worship bands, no high-tech presentations. It has always been about deep relationships.

Lately, however, Reyna has sensed a great deal of fragmentation and dysfunction. The teens act just fine at church, but she can feel their hurt, hidden behind a veneer of religiosity. She's not sure who the teens are anymore. During youth meetings they seem so spiritual, but she's been hearing stories of the same kids leading destructive, almost secret lives with their friends. "Where's the disconnect?" she wonders.

Reyna's not sure what to do with the incongruities. The students seem distant. It's like they don't trust her anymore. "What's going on?" She mutters. "I'm still me. Am I just getting older, or are the kids playing some sort of game?"

Reyna and Shaun are experiencing what a youth pastor friend of mine has dubbed "the new normal" and are unsure of their approaches. In this book, I hope to address the restlessness of many youth ministry workers today by taking an honest look at both youth culture and the theology that undergirds youth ministry.

Sweeping changes in the ways adults interact with young people are shaping the nature of adolescence itself. As we will see in chapter 1, adults are abandoning teens on their journey through adolescence. The adult world has become hostile territory in which teenagers survive rather than thrive. Broad cultural shifts in the ways teens think, believe, and understand life are altering the nature of youth ministry. They're reevaluating what truth is and how it can be experienced.

In the midst of these changes, Mike Yaconelli, a youth ministry innovator and leader, has charged that youth ministry as an experiment has failed.[2] If his assessment is true, youth ministry's demise has come in at least two ways. The first is the apparent inability of local youth ministries to carefully respond to their cultural contexts. The second is that the pragmatically-focused methods of most youth ministries, driven by what "works," lack theological depth and durability.[3] As a result, a durable faith is not really fostered in the typical youth group environment.

Admittedly, many young people today have developed a viable and vibrant faith. But the sad truth is that they are not the norm in many churches; they seem to be the exception. For all the resources and support accessible to youth workers today, youth work is not transforming young lives as it should. Maybe it's because much of contemporary youth ministry has become what I would call an "industry," a movement that emphasizes self-preservation more than ministry. As it has become institutionalized, youth ministry has become its own culture with a distinct social composition. As an industry, it has created a demand for resource suppliers and agencies that represent a sort of "franchising" of youth ministries.[4] Too many of us have become enamored with the trappings of the youth ministry industry. We're more in love with the idea of youth ministry than we are with the young people themselves.

There are two significant reasons for these struggles in contemporary youth ministry. First, our current models-driven youth ministry culture doesn't carefully consider the developmental task of today's adolescents nor does it reflect on the deeper levels of their cultural context. Chap Clark's concern is that youth workers do more theological, cultural, and developmental reflection "*on the fly* than through careful deliberation."[5] Second, there is an apparent theological deficiency in contemporary youth ministry. We need a more comprehensive and durable theology that directs and propels our practice. Authors such as Kenda Creasy Dean (*The Godbearing Life*) and Dean Borgman (*When Kumbaya Is Not Enough*) have written books to address this trend. Creasy Dean asserts that practical theology has been "altogether absent from the youth ministry equation."[6]

Too many youth workers, these authors fear, lack theological acumen and too few take their theology seriously. Youth ministry is a place in which adolescence, popular culture, and the gospel collide. In such a climate, youth workers must be good theologians to experience lasting effectiveness. Can they, will they rise to that challenge?

Pragmatics and "Models-Drivenness" in Youth Ministry

Contemporary youth ministry is models-driven, and continues to nurture a models-driven culture. Youth ministry models are everywhere.[7] From the youth ministry funnel of the 1980s and its inversion, the pyramid, to today's flagship model among evangelicals, purpose-driven youth ministry, youth workers flock to models, enamored of success stories and star power. Some have unique points, but most look and sound the same, just nuanced. Typically, youth ministry models separate the teens from adults in the congregation, focus on individual needs, and offer a personalized and private gospel.

The problem, however, is not the models themselves; many youth ministry models are helpful. What is disturbing is our eagerness to blindly adopt and apply successful, pre-packaged models, regardless of our context. In this way, so much of youth ministry has moved beyond models-usefulness to models-drivenness.

Think of it as a parallel to fads in food and nutrition. Notice how so many people latch onto the latest diet craze. Whether it's low-fat, low-carb, or juicing, thousands buy the books or the DVDs, expecting immediate and long-lasting results. After some initial success, the dieters slip back into old eating patterns and regain the weight.

Two forces are at work among dieters: the weight-loss strategy and the dieter's character. The success of any diet scheme depends on the persistence and willpower of the dieters. They must be determined to follow the plan, eat in moderation, and exercise regularly. The weight-loss strategy is only as effective as the character of the dieter. In the same way, a ministry model is only as effective as the theology in which it's rooted.

The current emphasis on ministry models reflects an evolution toward more sophisticated ministry methods.[8] Many youth ministries are moving away from informal, loosely structured meetings of fun and friendship. Instead they become highly developed, clearly focused, multi-layered, elaborate programs.

There are many positive sides to this trend. These programs can provide a compass for effective ministry. They embody a strategy to accomplish spiritual and numerical growth. Successful models offer structure and consistency. Some ministry activities that would otherwise seem strange can make sense when within the framework of a model. Tested youth ministry models are evaluative tools. In a constantly changing world, successful models remind us that God is still working in youth ministry.[9] They assure us that it is still possible to communicate the good news of Christ in a culturally relevant way.

Practical Pitfalls

Much as we love them, however, latching onto models has dangers and limitations. First, we can falsely assume that following a model somehow ensures ministry success, as if effective ministry cannot exist without a model. Clearly articulating and following a model, we assume, equals competent youth leadership. The most effective models are organically shaped, and evolve over time in response to the unique needs of particular ministry settings. Youth ministry innovators rarely set out to create a comprehensive model that will last for all time and work in every context. Generally, by the time a successful youth ministry model is marketed, it has experienced numerous evolutionary changes.

Still, models can be treated in a reductionistic way. Steve was a young, energetic, and gifted youth pastor in a small rural church. He was a passionate disciple of the Sonlife youth ministry model. Loosely based on the ministry practices of Jesus, Sonlife was (and still is) a proven ministry philosophy that had been around for years. However, after two years, Steve felt forced to leave his position and the teens for whom he cared so deeply. It wasn't because of the model itself, but because he was unwilling to adapt the model's philosophy to his particular context.

As Sonlife prescribed, Steve spent the vast majority of his time investing in the lives of a handful of student leaders, just as Jesus did with his disciples. For many of the teens however, this smacked of favoritism. Church leaders begged Steve to pay more attention to the at-risk students and those who were marginalized, which was also what Jesus did. Steve didn't flatly reject their appeals; he just subversively ignored them. His ministry strategy had no room for those ideas.

Eventually, the tension caused Steve to move on to greener pastures. Both sides—the church leaders and Steve—insisted they were in the right. But it was the teens who ended up being wronged.

As Steve's church found, pre-packaged, well-defined models run the risk of shrinking the ministry to a formula. They can also reduce adolescents and their needs to something less than the complex, beautiful, mysterious, and unique creations that they are. Rigidly applying a particular youth ministry model can render the ministry ineffective, unable to adapt to changing needs and situations.

This models-drivenness may be the most prevalent weakness of youth ministry today. When a popularized ministry model is applied without carefully adapting it to the particular ministry context, the way is prepared for the demise of the youth ministry. It has little to do with the model itself and more with a slavish application of the model.

A second limitation of a models-driven youth ministry culture is that celebrated models keep changing. Since the late 1970s, when youth ministry models were first identified,[10] so many new models have emerged and so many changes have been made that the '70s models are barely recognizable.[11] The noble, but sometimes desperate, attempt to be relevant and effective has youth leaders chasing the latest ministry fads. This undermines ministry continuity, and prevents certain strategies or programs from flourishing over time. It also frustrates teens and volunteers.

A third concern is that many of the trendy ministry models seem to be created in a vacuum. It's as if they're devised in a corner office, arising from a combination of what was probably some strategic thinking, careful reading, even prayer. But there's no real evidence that they've deeply engaged adolescent culture or the larger theology of Scripture.

The youth ministry funnel,[12] popularized by Duffy Robbins in the 1990s, has been replicated all across North America because of its simplicity and flexibility, but the theological and cultural issues aren't clearly addressed. Models like this look good on paper and make impressive presentations. But to what extent are they impacting lives? How seriously do they consider the emerging world of teens?

Where Are the Theological Foundations?

There are many practical dangers in trusting too strongly in models. But the most important danger is theological. Many of the popular ministry models don't adequately reflect biblical paradigms. In other words, they fail to capture God's bigger story as revealed in Scripture. While many models, such as Robbins' funnel, may be strategically sound, they present no clear understanding of the ways in which teens, youth ministries, and the church as a whole fit into the larger narrative of what God is doing in the world. While their influence comes from their simplicity and practicality—they really do work!—the models can be weak theologically.

In recent years, some of the better-known models, such as those of Sonlife[13] and Purpose Driven Youth Ministry,[14] have shown a stronger scriptural base than did earlier ones. They use Scripture texts (some more extensively than others) to support particular strategies or programs. Such models, including that of the Purpose Driven Youth Ministry, often purport to be rooted in biblical "principles." In fact, however, they are simply using Bible passages as proof texts to support externally imposed ideas or structures. (See discussion below.)

Even the use of these "principled" models can arise from a preoccupation with pragmatics. "Does it work?", a prevailing question in our culture, is also the persistent question running through the minds of most youth workers. A fixation on success, efficiency, and program management thus takes precedence over biblical faithfulness, effectiveness, and incarnational ministry.

I know that the workability of a youth ministry model is indispensable. Even so, practical concerns shouldn't be the primary shapers of our ministry strategies. Not only can they uproot ministry from the larger story of God; they may also fail to connect with the needs and aspirations of teens today. In essence, *Beyond Me* is an invitation to think about doing youth ministry in a way that is both effective and faithful. Young lives should be consistently transformed into the image of Christ through ministry methods that are faithful to the larger story of what God is doing.

Biblical Paradigms:
A Bigger Theology for Youth Ministry and for the Church

"This ring! . . . How did it come to me?"
"Ah!" said Gandalf. "That is a very long story."[15]

Frodo Baggins, the central character in Tolkien's classic fantasy trilogy, *The Lord of the Rings,* finds his life radically altered when he holds the One Ring in his trembling hobbit hands. At that moment, in his small Shire cottage, Frodo also takes his place in the bigger story of Middle Earth. Frodo's task is to cast the One Ring into the fires of Mount Doom to turn back the evil forces of Mordor. The future of Middle Earth is at stake.

Like Frodo, we in youth ministry need to rediscover the bigger story and call of Scripture, and to place ourselves and our youth within it. There is a larger gospel—a broader theology—that can shape our ministry strategies. As we have begun to see, pragmatically-driven youth ministry can be both effective and dangerous. Ministry models that are propelled by proof-texted biblical principles may have some theological footing, but they, too, are incomplete. They lack the capacity, force, and depth of a biblical paradigm.

Paradigms and principles are not the same thing. Biblical *paradigms* are built on more than one verse, passage, or contrived set of Scripture texts. They are recognizable themes woven throughout the entire biblical text. They can operate with multiple biblical categories (such as justice and shalom; or community, deliverance, and blessing). When held together, paradigms provide a more comprehensive way of reading life, ministry, and the world. Biblical paradigms are narrative in nature; they work toward integrating God's larger story revealed throughout the scope of Scripture.

Bible *principles*, on the other hand, tend to be distilled from a single text, with perhaps some corroborating evidence from other passages. They act more like proverbs than perspectives or ways of understanding. When it comes to youth ministry, principles tend to simplify and reduce. Today's teens are left wanting more. Youth ministry principles do not have the stature and breadth they need to integrate God's broader biblical agenda. Nor do they address the complexities of life, adolescence, and the world.

Let's consider Doug Fields' *Purpose Driven Youth Ministry* (PDYM), arguably the preeminent youth ministry strategy today. Fields believes that there are five eternal purposes for the church: evangelism, worship, fellowship, discipleship, and ministry[16] distilled from two primary biblical texts: the Great Commandment (Matthew 22:37-40) and the Great Commission (Matthew 28:19-20). Fields asserts that these purposes must be reflected in the overall mission of any youth ministry.

It would be hard to argue that these are not primary purposes of the church and essential components of youth ministry. However, analyzing this youth ministry model through the lens of a biblical paradigm reveals that PDYM is primarily rooted in *principles*, not a *paradigm*. The questions that come out of a bigger theological paradigm include the following: Are these principles the only purposes for the church? What about the ways in which the church responds to our world? How is the church serving as a witness to God's intended future for humanity: an alternative culture and an eschatological sign that bears witness to God's reign in the world? How does the church engage the world through compassion and suffering?

Looking through the lens of biblical paradigms raises other questions. Has Purpose Driven Youth Ministry been "principlized" in a way that resonates with a relatively affluent North American worldview? For instance, does the purpose of "evangelism" function solely at a personal level? Can evangelism also include the conversion from societal sins such as racism, classism, or consumerism?

Purpose Driven's tenets of "fellowship" and "discipleship" can seem to nurture a self-focused faith. Fellowship doesn't necessarily mean modeling a radically redeemed culture. Discipleship doesn't necessarily include promoting justice for the oppressed and marginalized. It even seems that the purpose of "ministry" is primarily an avenue of self-discovery.

I want to be very clear: the purposes of evangelism, worship, fellowship, discipleship, and ministry *are* biblically mandated principles. They're essential for church health. But the church is about so much more than a set of principled purposes. In a way that moves beyond these principles, the church is the primary agent for the breaking-in of God's reign in the world. The church's mission is part of God's ultimate goal in the world.

A youth ministry rooted in a biblical paradigm should not only be able speak to the issues of the church's purpose and how teens relate to it; it should also connect the teens' narratives to the story of God's people. It should address the way young people, as a part of a contrast faith community, engage the culture around them. Moreover, a biblical paradigm should invite adolescents to participate in God's purposes beyond the church, in the world.

Context, Theology, and Praxis: An Overview of This Book

To some youth ministry leaders, the experiment of youth ministry as we know it has failed. While the cause of its collapse is open to debate, I believe that a key factor has been a pragmatic focus that has led to a disconnect with the real world of today's adolescents, and an apparent lack of theological rootedness. Youth ministries must move beyond recent attempts at theological "principles." They must be driven by biblical paradigms that incorporate the depth, force, and trajectory of the gospel. They must address the complexities of adolescence, life, and the world.

Beyond Me proposes that God's reign (we'll also use the terms *kingdom* and *realm*) is a compelling theological paradigm that captures the multidimensional nature of the gospel. The kingdom of God, as a paradigm, can drive and guide youth ministry strategies that are biblically faithful and effective in our contemporary context.

"Narrative" is a motif that will run through this book. Our stories don't just tell of our pilgrimage through life—our litany of events and dates. They also speak of the influences that shape us. Relationships and experiences influence our stories, but so do much larger, hidden forces. World events, philosophies, societal shifts in our collective approach to life also nuance our narratives. Stories tell of who we are and who we are becoming.

Each of this book's two sections describes a narrative. Section One, "The Adolescent Narrative," focuses on the story of contemporary adolescents. Their narrative is structured with the framework of individuation, a primary psychosocial task of adolescence. As they journey toward adulthood, adolescents are wrestling with the essential questions: "Who am I?" "Where do I belong?" and "Do I really matter?" This section probes how the broader social forces of psychosocial abandonment, postmodernism, and the consumerist ideology of our culture shape adolescents' understanding of their narrative: their identity, belonging, and autonomy.

Section Two, "The Counternarrative of God's Reign" explores ways in which God's reign offers a contrast narrative. It considers God's reign as a biblical paradigm in its relational, narrative, transformational, and eschatological dimensions. These dimensions can powerfully "rescript" the contemporary adolescent narrative. Finally, this section offers some practical ideas for applying the paradigm to youth ministry. Beyond offering just another model, I propose a template for evaluating youth ministry models through a kingdom-driven grid.

This book represents a convergence of a variety of disciplines: adolescent development, teen culture, popular cultural analysis, biblical theology, and practical theology. Such integration is really what effective youth ministry is all about. We are called to understand who teens are developmentally, to pay attention to their social context, and to bring their culture into conversation with careful theology. Faithful praxis is the art of theological innovation and it is found at the intersection of context and theology.[17]

SECTION ONE

THE ADOLESCENT NARRATIVE

WIDE ANGLE

Framework	The Adolescent Narrative		
Individuation	Abandonment	Postmodernity	Consumerism
Identity *Who am I?*	Protracted—A longer search	Fragmented—Decentered self	Purchased—I am what I buy
Autonomy *Do I matter?*	Displaced—Not valued as unique creations of God	Abstracted—Who's the self that matters?	Commodified—Market-driven value
Belonging *How do I fit?*	Clustered—Found in peer clusters	Nomadic—Without a home	Branded—Brand affinity

one

The New Adolescent World: Identity, Autonomy, and Belonging

C ody's life as a fourteen-year-old high school student is normal, but it feels strange. How can life be so monotonous, exhilarating, and terrifying all at the same time? A lot has happened in the last year. He shot up in height, surpassing Mom and growing almost as tall as Dad. Even though his voice has deepened, he still squeaks and laughs like a sick donkey. "And where's all this hair coming from?" he wonders.

When Kelsey smiles at him as she walks down the hall, he feels a surge of something strange shooting through his body. His heart races and his stomach flutters. But the thought of even saying "Hi" to her sends chills up his spine.

Lately Cody has noticed that his parents seem to be getting stupider by the day. He wonders why he has to hang up his towel. He hates it when Mom makes him wear sunscreen. "I can fry if I want to," he mutters. In the mall he treats his family like perfect strangers to reduce the risk of humiliation. Mom and Dad, for their part, are frustrated by the emotional rollercoaster that Cody is riding. "So what if I'm goofy one minute and angry the next?" he thinks. "That's just the way I am."

Cody remembers the day he smelled his own stink. The stench was unbearable! He'd shower three times a day if he could. Only one pair of jeans looks good on him anymore. Every other pair is either too long, too short, too wide, or too stupid. Yesterday he had to wear a shirt and tie for a class presentation. "I look like an idiot," he cringed. "I know everyone's laughing at me."

Lately, Cody's been wondering about some huge questions. Who is he really—deep down? Where does he fit in the world around him? Do others really care about him and his choices? He's not sure about these things, and he's afraid to find out. And when will he finally know the answer to these questions? The thought just makes his brain hurt.

Cody is in the throes of adolescence. His body is changing. His hormones are surging and he doesn't know quite what to do with his changing role and relationship in the family. It's hard for Cody to get a handle on his emotions and he's finally internalizing the notion that other people notice him and have opinions about his appearance and behavior. Being cool is extremely hard work.

A vast array of variables makes Cody's adolescent journey unique, just as every other teen's story is different from all others. Heredity, social environment, family systems, and culture all blend to make Cody the person he is. But Cody shares some common characteristics with most other teens in North America. In our project of understanding how the story of God's reign can impact the life of teens, we must start with some basic understandings of the adolescent narrative today. That is the task of Section One of this book. And to begin understanding that narrative, this chapter examines the nature and context of contemporary adolescence in North America.

Individuation: The Adolescent Task

The term "adolescence" comes from the Latin word *adolescere* which means "to grow into," or "to grow toward." Another important term is "puberty" (*pubertas* in Latin), meaning "adult," or "adulthood." Generations ago, a young person was considered an adult at the onset of puberty. As we shall see, defining adolescence today is not as straightforward as it once was. But for our purposes, we will use the term to describe "the period of life between childhood and adulthood." Another helpful description would be the time frame beginning with biological adulthood and ending with societal adulthood.[1]

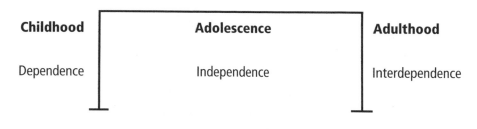

Figure 1. The Adolescent Tightrope

It may be helpful to picture this journey as a tightrope[2] (see figure 1). At the beginning of adolescence, around the onset of puberty (biological adulthood), a young person climbs onto the tightrope and inches carefully toward social adulthood. The tightrope illustrates the tenuous nature of the adolescent journey. As they shuffle along the tightrope, adolescents seek answers to questions of *identity* (Who am I?); *autonomy* (Do I or my choices matter?); and *belonging* (How do I fit into the world around me?) Adolescents become adults when culture affirms that they have individuated. This means that, according to the culture, these young people understand who they are, they are willing to take responsibility for their lives and choices, and they have entered interdependently into adult relationships. At this point, adolescents climb down from the tightrope.

During adolescence, young people are maturing physically, developing cognitively, and growing relationally and spiritually. At the heart of this growth is the psychosocial process of "individuation." During this journey of becoming an individual, adolescents grapple with three fundamental issues: identity, autonomy, and belonging.[3]

But as Cody and his peers are discovering, individuation is not just a solitary journey. Adolescents are wrestling with their self-understanding within a social context. Another metaphor that can help understand the process of individuation is that of lenses. In the movie *National Treasure*, Ben Gates (played by Nicholas Cage) finds a map located on the back of the United States Declaration of Independence.

With a set of spectacles he discovered along the way, Ben sees the map's outline. But it isn't until later that Ben reveals the treasure map's detail that was missing before. As Ben lowers different colored lenses in front of the glasses, new details begin to emerge. The map begins to make more sense and the vast treasure's location becomes clear.

Much like the spectacles Ben Gates uses to locate the national treasure, the process of individuation—answering the questions of identity, belonging, and autonomy—offers the primary lens through which adolescents see life and faith. Everything else (physical changes, cognitive development, social influences) functions like the colored lenses. While they have a significant impact on the life of an adolescent's developmental changes, they are processed through the primary lens of individuation.

What are the shapers of young people's sense of identity, belong-

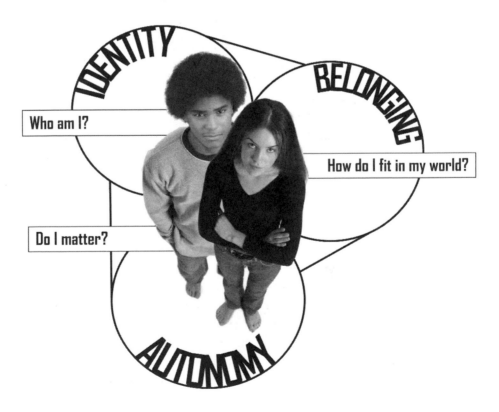

ing, and autonomy? First, as Christians we believe that this sense is constructed internally in adolescents as they hear the voice of God. They are uniquely created for a supreme purpose. They are created, gifted, chosen, and called by God.

But the discovery of this call does not occur in a vacuum. Family life, relationships, and experiences profoundly influence the ways in which teens construct their sense of individuality. Increasingly, adolescents are discovering their individuality in the context of community. As we shall see later in this book, this is where the congregation—the family of faith—can play a crucial role in both the social and faith development of youth.

At the same time, and perhaps most forcefully, adolescent individuality is influenced by the messages and symbols of the broader culture. Given its increasing influence and pervasiveness, the narrative of our North American culture must be taken seriously. Let us look at some of the key ways in which the broader culture today is shaping the sense of identity, autonomy, and belonging for our adolescents. One of the underlying realities in that culture, I believe, is the increasing abandonment of adolescents by adults.

Adult Abandonment

"I've been kidnapped. I have been taken from in front of my house. I'm in the back of a van. He put a gun to my head and he told me to run or he would shoot me and my family." These were sixteen-year-old Kelsey's first words in a frantic 911 call on an early April morning. Suddenly, a sleepy Kansas town was shaken. One of their own had been abducted at gunpoint.

Immediately, police issued an amber alert. Dozens of law enforcement people were mobilized. Townspeople feared the worst. Federal, state, and local officials were in a desperate search for the missing teen. Hundreds of local residents joined in the hunt. For hours there were no clues to Kelsey's whereabouts.

Then unexpectedly, after more than fifteen hours, Kelsey appeared on a friend's doorstep, out of breath and frightened. Somehow she had escaped her captor. She was home safe. Everyone breathed a collective sigh of relief.

But as she told the harrowing tale of her abduction, terror, and dramatic escape, details didn't add up. The FBI agents assigned to the case continued to question Kelsey about her mysterious disappearance. Finally, after ten hours of interviews, Kelsey broke. It was all a hoax, an extensive web of lies.

Family and friends stood by Kelsey in support, while other townsfolk were angry. Almost everyone was confused. Why? Why would Kelsey, a bright and cheerful, apparently well-adjusted teen, fake her own abduction? Friends admitted that she didn't seem like the type of person to do this. Kelsey's best friends, though baffled, believed that Kelsey "had her reasons" and affirmed that they were "behind her one hundred percent."

Since the incident, the family has been tight-lipped and the media hasn't seemed eager to find answers to this puzzling tale. But I believe Kelsey's story may give us a window into the world of today's adolescents. Kelsey herself confessed that she was an overachiever who experienced great pressure to perform. Pressure from whom? From studies of today's youth culture, we can conclude that any pressure she put on herself was probably a reaction to demands imposed on her by the adults in her world.[4]

If we would take the time to listen carefully to their stories, we would hear our teens consistently tell us of overwhelming pressure, of a semi-secret adolescent world, and of adult abandonment. In contrast to earlier generations, adolescence today is no longer the idyllic life phase in which teens dreamed, connived, and rebelled. Today, below the surface, teens harbor loneliness, fear, insecurity, stress, and strain as they try to survive a hostile world. Our society has turned away from its primary concern for its young. Today, North America's reputation as a child-centered culture is fading fast.[5] Instead, it is preoccupied with the dreams, needs, and stresses of adults, leaving adolescents in their own world.

When it was released, the movie *Napoleon Dynamite* was widely embraced among teens. Critics detested the film, but adolescents loved it. Why? One reason was that it portrayed an unpopular misfit finding wider acceptance while staying true to himself. But on a deeper look, one notices something else. Where are the adults? There is no mention of Napoleon's parents. He and his brother Kip live with their grandma. But she's out chasing her own dreams on the sand dunes until she injures herself in a dune buggy accident. The boys' Uncle Rico, who stays with them, only wants to make money and recruits Kip as an accomplice in his money-making capers. The school's principal doesn't want to see Napoleon and his friend Pedro succeed in the school's election. In the movie, no adults are really for the teens. Mostly, adults are either absent or hostile. Teens embraced the movie because it portrayed their adult-less adolescence so accurately. This abandonment is fast becoming the defining issue for today's adolescents.[6]

Adults, and the systems they create, have forsaken adolescents while the teens are still on the tightrope of individuation. Increasingly, they must negotiate the perils of growing up alone. Adult desertion has forced them to band together and create a world all their own—separate, semi-secret, and vastly different from the world around them."[7]

To claim that adult systems have abandoned adolescents, however, is not to assert that they have abandoned them physically or materially. As a group, today's teens in North America have access to billions of dollars in disposable spending each year.[8] The abandonment they experience is a *psychosocial* abdication. Adults have walked away from adolescents emotionally and socially on their journey toward adulthood. One of the consequences of this abandonment, according to a forward-looking 1995 report by the Carnegie Council on Adolescent Development, is that society is neglecting its young adolescents to such an extent that half of them may be irrevocably damaging their chances for productive and healthy futures.[9]

Not all observers would describe our teen culture in terms of abandonment. Some argue that today's adolescents are more stable and healthy than ever before.[10] Their academic and creative achievements are remarkable. And so many teens have demonstrated a striking resilience in overcoming the difficulties of dysfunctional family systems.

But could it be that both views are complementary—in an eerie sort of way? On the *surface* the adolescents appear to be doing very well. But beneath the calm waters of all the optimistic empirical data there is much more going on in the lives of today's teens than most adults realize. Remember the contradictions in Kelsey's story: a struggling adolescent hiding behind the facade of high achievement. Many teenagers are dealing with enormous pressure from coaches, teachers, and parents to excel. Often, the result is an unhealthy performance orientation in which they comply with adult demands more out of their fears than out of an innate sense of purpose. Many adolescents appear to have life all together, but beneath their cool exterior, there's more hurt than we would care to admit.[11]

Evidence of Abandonment

Family systems. The emotional center of the contemporary family has shifted from the child to the adult. The sentimental feelings that attach us to one another are now more likely to favor the well-being of the adults. For example, children are passed around between acquaintances, family members, and childcare agencies while their parents are working two jobs and taking classes on the side. Teens in these family systems assume undue household management responsibilities; they are forced to juggle the realities of family stress alongside the perils of adolescence. This shift, therefore, requires an increased level of self-sacrifice from the young.

The value of family togetherness has been replaced with autonomy. Family members are encouraged to place their needs for self-fulfillment ahead of the family unit. And since adults are the more forceful and authoritative contributors to the family system, this need imbalance favors the adults in charge. If both parents need to work sixty- to eighty-hour weeks to achieve certain career goals, so be it. In this environment, teenage children are encouraged to handle life's complexities—from homework to heartbreak—on their own.

When the concerns and well-being of children consistently come second, young people are forced to adopt survival strategies. As they're able to reflect on their family situations, adolescents come to grips with the reality that they are on their own. And because adults now treat them as more sophisticated mini-adults, many teens experience little support during their adolescent journey. In this survival mode, they experience a deep sense of aloneness and abandonment. As Kelsey's acting out illustrates, this feeling has led to increasingly self-destructive behaviors and habits that David Elkind groups together under the heading, "the new morbidity."[12] As our culture sends its young people into an adult world ill-equipped to navigate its mounting demands, more and more of them are experiencing a deep inner sense of lostness.[13]

Cultural conditions. Signs of abandonment appear not only in the family, but also in the broader culture. A quick look at newer subdivisions, for example, reflects a sense of isolation. Without sidewalks connecting homes, newer subdivisions are not built to nurture close neighborhood relationships. Residential streets, both old and new, may be populated with children, but few adults are visible. With increasing class sizes and hectic course schedules, students are less able to have meaningful, unhurried conversations with teachers. For social activities, teens are more or less on their own, partying in adult-free environments. Busier lives have forced many families to spend less downtime together.

The isolation is reflected in the fading of cultural markers that provide adolescents with a sense of becoming. For instance, the value and meaning in graduating from high school or in getting a driver's license have been diminished. Moving on to college or being able to drive is not necessarily a significant indicator of progress toward maturity.

A generation ago, such markers helped define a special place for adolescents. The way teens dressed, the activities in which they participated, or the information and messages they were allowed to absorb (for example, in movies) all helped to create a teenage niche. Now, the lines between generations are blurring. Both children and grownups are looking and acting more and more like teens. So what makes one's adolescence unique?

Teenage culture, which emerged in the 1920s, is already disappearing. The meaning infused in adolescent markers, such as going to dances, playing organized sports, or dating, is being erased. Many of those activities are no longer unique to teens because younger children already participate in them. These vanishing markers contribute

The short history of our society's understanding of adolescence as a life stage shows how much of a cultural invention it is. As a result of G. Stanley Hall's research at the turn of the twentieth century, adolescence was recognized as a subculture by the 1920s. It wasn't embraced as a legitimate stage of life, however, until the 1960s. By the 1970s adolescence was understood to begin at the age of thirteen and end at eighteen. As we see below, those age parameters have widened, indicating that a culture's markers shape both the length of adolescence and the nature of teens' experience of it.

to adolescent abandonment by obscuring the special place our culture has for teenagers. Without this unique place, adolescents have been handed a premature adulthood that they do not altogether embrace. Without the internalized rules, limits, and expectations that cultural markers create, teens are often forced to make age-inappropriate decisions. This only adds to a growing sense of pressure and abandonment.

The Adolescent Perception of Abandonment

Perhaps the most compelling evidence of abandonment is the sense of neglect that adolescents themselves feel. In his 2004 study, Chap Clark discovered an alarming trend.[14] High school age teens clearly and increasingly feel abandoned by adult systems. When they get to high school most teens have been subjected to years of adult-driven and adult-controlled institutions and relationships. Adult systems can be organizations, institutions, or relationships that are primarily concerned with achieving adults' agendas, needs, and dreams. They are for and about the adults in charge.

Take education, for example. When schools are more preoccupied with gaining financial benefits on the basis of student test scores than with student learning, they have become an adult system. Students then learn to play to adult expectations. As they mature, adolescents intuitively discern that adult systems are not designed to nurture them. This is when they first sense the need to survive. Adolescents have figured out that the safest route through school with minimal adult intrusion is doing exactly what the teacher wants. Don't ask too many questions, don't appear too eager, and do whatever it takes to get the kind of grades that will prevent parental interference.

Or think about the youth sports machine. Whom is it for? Does it exist so children and young teens can have fun playing a sport that teaches them valuable life lessons? Or is it about the coach's win/loss record, or about parents' needs to live vicariously through their children, pushing them to athletic excellence no matter the cost. When I hear of parents resorting to fist fights over a team's miserable performance, it seems to be about the adults. When a coach pays a player to throw a baseball at an autistic teammate's head so that the weaker player is scratched from the game's roster, I know the sport is no longer for the youth.[15] Not all coaches or parents fit this pattern, of course, yet the incidents suggest that youth sports are tilting toward being an expression of adult systems, increasing the alienation between adults and youth.

Clark has found that the absence of meaningful relationships with adults has led to an overwhelming sense of loss among teens.[16] In my own conversations with teens and youth ministry professionals from around the United States and Canada I have heard resounding agreement with this bleak assessment. I hear comments like, "Abandonment is our reality, and adults have no idea." High school counselors and youth pastors have repeatedly told me, "This gives a name to something I've been seeing for a long time." This growing isolation among adolescents easily breeds cynicism and mistrust. It widens the chasm between the two realities of the pressure-filled adult realm and their adolescent refuge of relational safety.

Hovering Adults and Abandonment

Many culture watchers and youth leaders argue that the current, and growing, phenomenon of "helicopter parents"[17] challenges the claim that teenagers are really abandoned. These parents are the engaged moms and dads who hover over their kids. They orchestrate a frenetic schedule of ballet lessons, soccer practice, and youth symphony concerts for their kids, and they're more than willing to accompany them to all these activities.

Surely this busyness can't be abandonment, can it? Let's take a closer look. These parents often see their children as extensions of themselves, making anxiety today's hallmark of both parenting and growing up. Generally, parents are much more demanding of their children than they were of themselves at that age. They expect better grades, better behavior, and more accountability. Any potential downtime is filled with more busyness. Essentially, helicopter parents are overly investing their egos in their children's performance. Their children complete them. As someone once quipped, it's almost "narcissism by proxy."

If we had to choose, wouldn't it be better to be in a family of overly-involved, hovering parents than in one where parents are completely absent? At least on some levels, the behavioral outcomes of the teens in such families are probably more positive, with higher academic achievement, a stronger goal-orientation, and reduced levels of substance abuse.[18] Yet there are hidden consequences that are not so positive. These family systems consist of enmeshed relationships that keep teens from exercising a healthy sense of autonomy, a vital feature of growing up. If you ask a "helicoptered" teen about her family life, a likely response would be: "I feel smothered. Let me out of here!" While teens with little parental involvement have almost no boundaries, children of helicopter parents may have too many boundaries.

In family systems with hovering parents, stress levels are high and trust levels are low. The children are striving to meet their parents' demands for a strong performance, whether it's in school, sports, or even church. It's not uncommon to hear teens decrying the unrealistic expectations burdening them.[19] The stress and fragmentation of life is stuffed inside, hidden behind a cool exterior. Like Kelsey, the teens don't want to let their parents down, but they're afraid to express their feelings in dealing with these pressures. I've known families in which parents' over-involvement drives teens underground in living out taboo escapades. The stakes of being honest about life are too high, so the teens become highly skilled in duplicity as they chart their courses for survival. Individually at least, teens have now almost universally sanctioned lying, deception, and protection as a way to control their environment.[20]

I believe this helicopter phenomenon, driven by adult agendas, is also a form of abandonment. It may even be more insidious because the abandonment is so subtle. After all, pressure-packed activities encouraged by hovering parents are cloaked in the language of love and care. Activity is understood as nurture and organizational involvement presented as love. In the process, parents are losing the ability to nurture their children. Like absent parents, they are primarily concerned with their own agendas rather than the welfare of their children. The fundamental question is, "Whom is this for?" If the parenting agenda is intended to accomplish adult concerns with little regard for adolescent needs, it is a form of abandonment.

Consequences of Abandonment

A culture of adult abandonment of teens has resulted in a number of other phenomena that must be taken into account in any theology and practice of youth ministry today. Among the consequences, let's look at three important ones: extended adolescence; peer clustering; and the preference to live separate from the adult world.

A longer adolescence. Not long ago, I ran into Matt, a recent college graduate with degrees in music and graphic design. Matt was bright and articulate with a lot going for him. I was surprised to see him working as a part-time groundskeeper at the college. I asked him what his future plans were. With a twinkle in his eye and a coy grin he whispered, "I have no idea. I just know that I'm in no hurry to start that adult thing."

Matt is not alone. Increasingly, college grads are opting for interim paths such as internships, short-term mission assignments, or travel before they dive into the trappings of careers and adult roles. Even the media markets this image. Remember the twenty-something couch potato? He loafs around the house, mooching off his parents who finally ask, "What do you think this is, a Holiday Inn?" That image was funny because the notion of an adult living at home was so rare it was comical. Now, years later, it's becoming the norm. Watch how advertisers market the image of the juvenile adult male stuck in some sort of adolescent time machine. Similarly, pay attention to how marketers play to the women who are still searching for an idyllic adolescence and innocence that has somehow slipped away.

Demographic patterns confirm the picture. The transition to adulthood now occurs over a longer period of time than was the case during the middle of the twentieth century. Contemporary adolescence is a passage without a clear endpoint. What was once seen as a

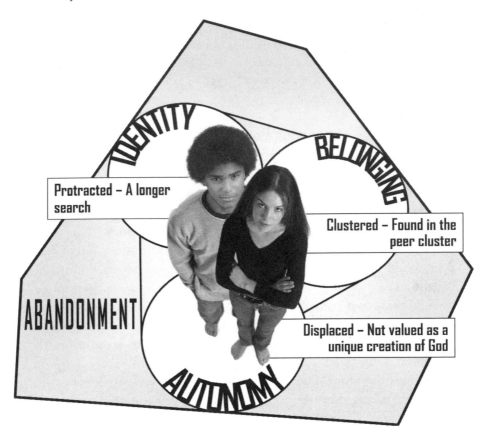

Protracted – A longer search

Clustered – Found in the peer cluster

Displaced – Not valued as a unique creation of God

IDENTITY

BELONGING

ABANDONMENT

AUTONOMY

five-year process in the 1970s (ages thirteen to eighteen) has now become a twelve- to fifteen-year journey (ages twelve to the mid-twenties). The degree to which adolescents are adequately able to answer questions around individuation determines the length and quality of their adolescence. Especially in a culture that is ambivalent about helping teens sort out their identity, the process of individuation is taking longer than ever before.

As adolescence has lengthened, its journey has also become more complex. Until recently, adolescence was described as *early* and *late*. Now a new phase has emerged: *middle* adolescence. Early adolescence begins at eleven or twelve years of age and continues until about the age of fourteen. Late adolescence has now been pushed back to begin at about age eighteen and continue unto the mid-twenties.[21] A new stage, middle adolescence, fills the space between fourteen and eighteen years of age. Only now are we beginning to discover the unique needs and activities of young people in the second stage.[22]

During middle adolescence, teens do not see family support as a significant point of security. Time spent with parents is not as important as a simple assurance that parents are available and want to be present. Middle adolescents become more aware of their need to be on their own, apart from family. This means more time with friends and a desire to make their own choices. Consequently, the self-focused nature of adolescence in this phase negatively affects family cohesion.

The emergence of middle adolescence is important to youth ministry because high school-aged teens, to whom most youth ministry strategies are geared, are no longer *late* adolescents on the edge of adulthood. They are still in the throes of individuation. Most senior high students in youth ministry are nowhere near the cusp of identity achievement and maturity. In many ways they are further behind in the maturing process than adolescents were, say, in the 1980s.

The phenomenon of clusters. Friends mean the world to Stephanie, a sixteen-year-old in high school. "My friends are the only people who really know me," she says. Stephanie enjoys the suburban life her parents have worked hard to provide for her, and she does well enough in school. But something is missing. Her career-driven parents have little time for Stephanie now. They rarely eat meals together. Stephanie's teachers and coaches just keep piling on the pressure and no one seems to want to listen. No *adult*, that is. Instead, Stephanie's friends are her life. Her circle of friends is a tightly knit group. They're at the mall together, and they hang out at each others' homes. They laugh and cry together. They make their way through the pressures of school and try to understand boys together. On the surface her friendships seem like typical, fun-loving, boy-crazy adolescent relationships. But they're much more than that. For Stephanie, friends are necessary to maneuver through the minefields of the complex and dangerous life of adolescence.

In years past, adolescent culture had a coherent center: the "in" group. Everyone else looked on longingly toward that group of star athletes, cheerleaders, and other popular teens. The rest evaluated themselves on the basis of their proximity to the "in" group. Today, adolescent culture is a web or network of clusters without a coherent center. The idea of "in" or "out" has little to do with adolescent culture as a whole. It has more to do with particular clusters.

This adolescent social construct of "clusters" is at the heart of being young today. It provides a place to belong.[23] While the character of clusters may vary in terms of gender, the motivation for these tight-knit peer groups is the same: survival. Teens, sensing the psychosocial abandonment of adults, begin forming clusters in early adolescence, but they begin to solidify during the second year of high school. Until life after high school begins to dissolve the cluster's cohesion, the groups play a family-like role. In the cluster, teens sense the relational closeness and safety that was once the hallmark of the family system. In fact, many adolescents feel a greater degree of presence, emotional support, and trust in the cluster than they do in their own families. The bond of the cluster is almost tribalistic.

Most clusters are usually gender-specific groups of four to ten teens. They are politically aligned with some other clusters, but in conflict with others. Loyalty to the cluster is the highest value. The norms of the cluster are intuitively negotiated as it is being formed, and they continue to evolve throughout its life. Personal values and ethics become subordinate to those of the cluster.

The urgent sense of self-protection has significantly increased the level of intimacy in today's peer clusters. The survival-focused cluster has more say over teen activities and attitudes than the activity-centered cliques of yesteryear. As a result, adolescents build close peer relationships with those who share similar self-concepts and can provide them with a degree of safety and a sense of trust. If a young person tries to find support and friendship from someone with a stronger self-concept she will usually feel socially and emotionally inferior, negating the purpose of the friendship. On the other hand, if she forms a bond with someone with a weaker self-concept, she will feel dragged down by that other person.[24]

Clusters do not form around purposes of amusement or social status. What clearly drives a middle adolescent to the cluster is an intuitively felt urgency to survive the adult world, which has become aloof from them. Parents, teachers, and coaches all seem to clearly communicate their expectations of teens, but rarely take time to listen to them and understand them. So adolescents comply in order to survive; their appearances in the adult world may even look confident and enthusiastic. But their real desire is to relate in the safety of their cluster.

Clustering has significant implications for youth ministry. Almost all current youth ministry strategies, rooted in the 1970s, still assume that teens organize themselves around a central, "in" group. Whether or not that assumption was ever healthy, the balance of power has not only shifted; it has dissipated. The "in" groups, such as the athletes, the cheerleaders, and the more popular students no longer dominate the culture. Clustering seems to be moving teen social structures toward a web of less coherently related sub-sets of tight-knit friendship groups formed on the basis of relational trust and safety. In youth ministry, we need to create new methods to work within, and capitalize on, the reality of clusters.

Secret living in a world beneath. Not long ago at a conference in Los Angeles, I spoke with Jason, a youth pastor from central California. He told me a story about Caleb, a vocal leader in his youth group. Caleb served on the youth worship team and helped start a guys' Bible study called "Wild Truth." He was outspoken about his faith and was planning to be a student guide on a summer mission trip to Mexico.

As the mission trip approached, another student urged Jason to check out what Caleb had been posting on the social networking site MySpace.com, a cyber combination of yearbook, personal diary, and social club. What Jason found was both shocking and appalling. After viewing a few explicit images and reading his angry blog, Jason couldn't believe that the Caleb on MySpace was the same Caleb he knew in youth group.

When Jason confronted Caleb about what he found, Caleb blew it off. "I was just having fun," he said. "It's no big deal." But then Caleb turned on Jason. "What gives you the right to nose around in my world?" he growled. "I thought I could trust you."

As this incident shows, the widening the gap between the adult world and that of adolescents and their clusters has helped nurture a youth system that operates invisibly beneath the surface and apart from the sphere of adult systems.

Teens quickly realize that, for years, they've been subjected to all sorts of adult systems. Home, school, work, sports—even youth group—are perceived as adult systems that don't really have the best interests of the young people at heart. As a result, adolescents start operating in layers. Above the surface, observable to adults, is the adult world driven by adult systems. Since they sense the adult world to be hostile, this is where teens "play the game," and learn how to "beat the system" into which adults have forced them. Adolescents are just trying to survive the adult world.

Then there is the layer *beneath*, where adolescents really want to be. Here they find a place of relational safety where the primary behavioral code is loyalty. This underground world is more pervasive and separate than ever before. Those who recognize the significance of abandonment are finding that the cyber community of teens found on journal hosting and social networking websites like MySpace and Facebook provide evidence of this layered living.

Such practices of survival, especially evident during midadolescence, have created a relational barrier between the adult world and the adolescent "underworld." Imagine a town under siege during a relentless bombing campaign. Townspeople bunk underground where they feel most safe. They only come to the surface out of necessity. When the townspeople are above ground, their activities and actions are radically different from those in their underground refuge. Scurrying, they gather food and water while avoiding injury or death. Sometimes looting or bribery is necessary. Underground is where the families hold each other, tell stories, sing, and dance. All the while, bombs may continue to explode in the other world, on the surface. This is similar to the way in which midadolescents operate. The insidious adult world above is something they must survive; the ethic of survival in the world below guides their behaviors and choices.

This idea hit close to home at the dinner table one evening. My teenage son, sharing his highs and lows of the day, muttered that he went "out" in the second round of his middle school's spelling bee. I was surprised because Taylor is an avid reader and a very good speller.

We asked him what word he misspelled. "Mustard," he said.

"How did you spell it," I asked. Taylor spelled "M-U-S-T-E-R-D."

"Well, how *do* you spell it?"

"M-U-S-T-A-R-D" was his immediate response.

"You threw the spelling bee?" I bellowed.

Shelly, in that typical mothering tone, affirmed him. "Taylor, we're proud of you no matter what happens."

"Wait," I barked. "You took a dive in the second round?"

"Relax Dad," he snapped, "Everyone does it!"

That was an epiphany for me. Even a spelling bee is seen as a part of an adult system. It's a chance for every student but one to experience public failure. I could just imagine how, as Taylor sat down, his friends would have glanced his way with a wink and a nod. "We all know you're smarter than that." The students who are more socially aware or less aggressive have learned to play the game, to survive and save a little face along the way.

Once we understand that they are operating with the ethic of survival, the midadolescent "world beneath" makes more sense. Feeling anonymous and powerless in a world devoted to the concerns of adults—whether at school or in the family—the teens now find their own ways to try to nurture their needs for belonging and identity. [25]

The world of teen sex, for example, reflects a desire for intimacy, relationship, and a safe place, easing an intense feeling of loneliness. It provides an exciting experience and satisfies their desire for adventure. Similarly, the adolescent party scene may be more about strengthening a sense of community than anything else. This could be where the tribalistic nature of the world beneath is most evident. For most teens, these memorable events are not so much about the drinking, drugs, music, or sex as about a sense of common history, community, and belonging.

To adults, the ethical grid in this world beneath appears inconsistent and self-centered. It looks like relativistic ethical opportunism.

But let's remember, adolescent behaviors and choices are generally filtered through the lenses of self-interest and self-protection. Adolescents are trying to navigate the complexities of life alone. Their preoccupation with creating an easier, safer, and more satisfying world drives their decisions and actions.

Youth Ministry as an Adult System

We in youth ministry are not immune to perpetuating the adult system that abandons youth. Teens are trying to survive our programs, too. This revelation came clear to me a few years ago at a national youth convention in Estes Park, Colorado, at which I was the emcee. On the last night, our speaker offered the typical youth conference invitations to commitment. The first was to acknowledge Jesus as Lord and Savior for the first time. Of the 1,500 students there, I saw a dozen teens stand to their feet.

The second invitation was to "recommit" their lives to Christ, to start over again with renewed spiritual passion and energy. There was a huge commotion as youth shot to their feet. They stood so quickly that I thought I felt a gust of wind rushing toward the rafters of the auditorium. From where I stood backstage, I saw no teen seated.

Continued on page 45

Abandonment and the Adolescent Narrative

In this chapter we have examined the ways in which adult abandonment has increased the complexity, pressure, and confusion of adolescence. Now let's revisit the crucial adolescent task of individuation. How does abandonment script today's adolescent narrative? As the chart on page 24 outlines, adolescents are asking questions of identity, autonomy, and belonging: "Who am I?" "Do I matter?" and "How do I fit in my world?" What kind of answers are they getting?

A protracted search for identity. Today's adolescents are struggling to find a healthy self-identity without a supportive adult scaffold or structure of standards and values.[26] They may initially look to the grown-ups around them for help, but many of those adults are focused on their own agendas, stressed and stretched to the brink. So, without a significant adult presence to help teens test and explore their identity, adolescent individuation becomes a long, drawn-out search.

The ministry challenge is to find ways to help adolescents hear the voice of God. Teens need to understand that they are unique creations of God, called to bring God's hope and healing to the world. Perhaps the most effective response we can make to the culture of abandonment is to relate to teens without the baggage of our self-focused adult agendas.

We must also understand that we can help our

youth find their identity within Christian community.[27] Adults in the church can be intentional about how the faith community shapes the identity of their teens. As we surround adolescents with love and affirmation, telling the larger story of God's reign, we form a contrasting community through which teens come to understand themselves and their world.

Displaced autonomy. Healthy adolescent autonomy emerges with a rising sense of personal legitimacy which, in turn, is informed by a growing sense of value. Along the way teens look for someone, anyone who communicates, "You matter to me." But often, the reality is that their sense of value is a qualified one, and as a consequence their sense of autonomy is also compromised. Grown-ups tend to validate teens whose choices and behaviors most benefit the interests of the adults in charge. Adolescents don't believe they're accepted and valued as the beautiful, mysterious, unique creations that they are. Their value has been displaced. Consequently, young people tunnel further into their world where they feel authenticated by other teens.

As youth workers, do we recognize the enormous opportunity we have to contribute to adolescent autonomy? Youth need us to accept them without the qualifiers of our adult agendas and expectations. When we value teens as unique individuals created in God's image, their sense of autonomy can blossom because, maybe for the first time, they are surrounded by adults who validate them for who they are.

Clustered sense of belonging. Because of abandonment, a sense of belonging, for most contemporary adolescents, is not necessarily found in family bonds, academic endeavors, or athletic teams. They sense that their place is with their peers in the safety of the peer cluster.

Continued from page 44

My evaluation must be taken with a grain of salt. God may have been working in ways too powerful for me to grasp. Still, I have attended too many youth camps and conferences over the last twenty years not to notice this new reality: the invitation to recommitment goes out and almost all the adolescents stand almost instantaneously. Could it be that even our well-planned youth conference was just another adult system?

At such conferences as the one I hosted, the most dangerous response for an adolescent is to stay seated. She'll have all sorts of adults hounding her for that decision. What's the safest thing to do? Just stand. That's what we adults want, isn't it? For the invitation to first-time decision, some intense interaction with adults might be called for, but not with the call to recommitment. Just a few hugs and everyone leaves with a warm fuzzy feeling.

In youth ministry we must first acknowledge the degree to which we may have contributed to the perceived hostility of an adult world where teens exist to serve the interests of adults. We must also tap into teens' deep longing for safety and loyalty. So the question becomes, "How can we make our ministry programs and relationships safe enough for teens to genuinely explore Christ, life, and themselves?" The safer teens feel, the more trust grows. And as trust develops, they're more likely to feel a sense of belonging in the church.

I remember taking my son Taylor to a "preparation for manhood" ceremony. He and a few other twelve-year-old boys from our congregation were blindfolded and brought to the shore of a nearby lake. I led Taylor toward a crackling fire. Against the night, the flames illuminated the faces of about a dozen men and their older sons. The ceremony began with an off-key, but rousing rendition of the hymn, "Rise Up O Men of God." Next, several men in the church, including the fathers of the boys, shared their wisdom on a wide range of topics: spiritual life, godly relationships, and sexual purity. Into a bag each man placed an object that symbolized their advice. The men blessed and prayed for each boy.

On the way home, Taylor and I stopped at a restaurant for a bite to eat and a conversation about what it means to be a godly man. I wish I could say that our conversation was life-changing, but I can't. Yet it was important to me that Taylor knew there was a crowd of caring adults that embraced him and cared deeply about his spiritual journey and his growth toward adulthood.

This is just one way the church can model broader adult support for adolescents on that vital journey of individuation. Youth ministries can come alongside teens as they ask their questions about identity. They can emphasize community, a value to which adolescents are predisposed in their quest to belong. As they are integrated into the body of Christ as fully functioning contributors who exercise their particular gifts, they also demonstrate autonomy.

two

Life on the Other Side: Working with Postmodern Culture

Luke has been in youth ministry a little over a year now and it is not exactly what he expected. At the beginning, he felt ready for the highs and lows and the daily grind of the job. Since he is a young adult in his twenties, he thought he was fairly in touch with adolescent culture, but now his teens have made him rethink his ability to connect with them.

Luke first noticed something during a devotional about the teachings of Jesus. He detected some curled lips, raised eyebrows, and apparent smirks when he said that Jesus was the only way to heaven. Also, several students had been requesting a study on other religions—not to refute them, but because of a genuine interest in other beliefs.

It was becoming obvious that many of the teens craved a more tangible worship experience. They thought and talked about God a lot, but not in the way their parents did. They were unsure about the formal church thing with its individualized faith orientation. The students kept insisting that their faith is more personal and communal. Luke was surprised by their sense of unity. They were making life choices—even faith decisions—together. Luke was all for unity and oneness, but this was more than he expected.

The real shocker came when one of the teenagers, Jordan, shook Luke's ministry to its core. Jordan had been consistently attending an in-depth Bible study, and was asking good questions. He had gone on the most recent mission trip to San Antonio and had shown real spiritual growth.

Luke had considered asking Jordan to serve on the ministry team. But now Luke discovered that Jordan was actively involved in a group that practiced principles of some Eastern religions. When Luke confronted Jordan about what seemed to be some inconsistencies, Jordan responded, "What contradictions?" What was going on with his students? What influences are making them act and think this way?

In recent years, our culture has experienced a noticeable shift. By rejecting absolute notions of truth and objectivity in favor of subjective truths, our culture has drifted from a prevailing worldview of modernism to one often referred to as postmodernism. Since its emergence, postmodernism has been controversial in the church. Some, like theologian and futurist Leonard Sweet, embrace it, arguing that the church needs to get in front of the cultural and intellectual shifts. The church's job now is "to hoist the sail and catch God's wave."[1] Others flatly reject postmodernism. Philosopher and professor Doug Groothius argues that it is very bad news philosophically, ethically, apologetically, and theologically.[2]

While Sweet and Groothius fall on opposite ends of the spectrum, they appear to agree that postmodernism is here and is shaping the world in which we now live. The question for us is, "How do we engage this emerging worldview in a way that is effective and yet faithful to Scripture?" In youth ministry we must be keenly aware of postmodernism's influence on adolescents and how it shapes their narrative. In this chapter we will define postmodernism, discuss how we can recognize it in our teens and, more specifically, understand how it shapes the adolescent narrative. Then we will briefly outline ways in which youth ministry can respond to postmodernism.

What Is Postmodernism?

Postmodernism, by nature, is difficult to define, but we can describe it. As the term suggests, it represents a quest to critique and move beyond modernism.[3] To better explore its meaning, therefore, it helps to contrast it with modernism. Modernism presupposes that there is objective truth that is discernable, knowable, and testable. Our task as humans is to understand that truth. Postmoderns, on the other hand, believe that, since it is impossible to be absolutely objective about truth, we should be suspicious of declarations of universal truth to which we all are subject. "How can anyone make such claims with absolute certainty?" ask postmoderns, concluding that truth is relative to one's personal understanding.

With postmodernism, therefore, we are seeing a shift in how life, the world, and reality are explained. Postmodern philosophy has moved from "metanarrative"—a grand, epic story that tells "an overarching tale about the world"[4]—to the local narrative. The modern understanding of metanarrative assumes that absolute truth can be known with absolute objectivity. The knowledge of this truth not only makes sense out of life, it can unite humanity and lead us to Utopia, the state of social perfection. But postmoderns reject the modern metanarrative because of its universal pretensions, its claims to be "the ultimate theory of everything."[5]

This shift is expressed in the principle of deconstructionism, which questions traditional assumptions about certainty, identity, and truth. In many ways it attempts to unmask our belief systems and expose them for what they really are: our own constructions of reality.[6] Deconstruction has led to a shift in how truth is validated. Modernism leaned heavily on scientific discovery as the primary way to verify truth. Scientific theory begins with the assumption of doubt; everything must be proven to be true. One can only trust what testing can substantiate. Postmodernism, by contrast, would argue that lived experience is the highest form of truth. Experienced truth goes beyond that which can be tested in a lab. Lived truth cannot be refuted.

Both deconstruction and the emphasis on experience are informed by the postmodern tenet of subjectivism. Reality cannot be objectively known, postmoderns argue, because we all observe it through arbitrary lens. No one can lay claim to absolute objectivity, something Leonard Sweet refers to as "immaculate perception."[7]

The role of self and its relationship to others has also shifted. Modernism championed the autonomous self. During the

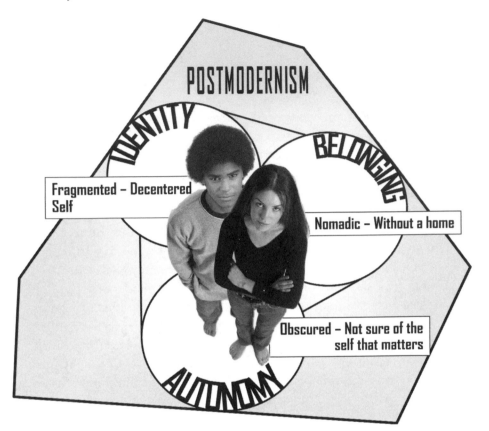

Enlightenment of the sixteenth century, philosopher Rene Descartes declared, "I think, therefore I am." Modernism endorsed the thinking that "the individual knower was higher and more pure than a group of knowers."[8] But postmodernism is suspicious of individual truth claims; one size does not necessarily fit all. While individuals can know truth, they cannot know all truth—and they can't know it with objectivity. With postmodernism, therefore, has come a shift toward community. People need others to help them understand life and the world, to help them construct a more durable map of reality.

Finally, our cultural mood has shifted. Modernism carried a feeling of human triumph and the optimism of progress. The project of modernism was to master nature and to perfect the human condition. This would eventually lead to Utopia. But postmoderns ask, "With all of the scientific, medical, and technological advances of the modern era, shouldn't Utopia be here by now? Look at the wars around the world, the genocide, AIDS, and global starvation. Are we really better off?" They assert that the modern project has failed. Modern optimism has given way to a sense of cynicism, even misery.

Postmodernism has brought significant changes in the way many people view and experience truth, human "progress," and relationships. We're now living on the other side in a new cultural paradigm. And, sure enough, postmodernism is becoming increasingly evident in today's teens. There isn't one teen or youth ministry context that hasn't been touched in some way by postmodern thinking. The following are some reflections on how it is influencing their narrative and what it might mean for youth ministry. (Also, refer back to page 24's "Wide Angle" for an outline of the key issues.)

Postmodernism, the Adolescent Narrative, and Youth Ministry

The postmodern shift has altered the ways in which our culture understands what is really real. Postmodernism assumes that truth and reality are understood or mediated through our own lenses. Life is just a personal production. Anytime a lens of some sort is used, there is distortion of some kind. So, the thinking goes, there's no overarching truth or reality outside of ourselves. That's because there's no way we can ascertain the truth in its purest form. What is really real? We can't know for certain.

This kind of thinking, taken to its logical end, can make the world a scary place. If we can't know what's really real, is it possible that there is no reality beyond ourselves, beyond our limited perspectives and knowledge? Is it possible that there is no real home in which we live? Furthermore, is it possible that the "me" I've come to know is also some kind of invention—an identity formulated through my own lenses? Without a firm reality to call home and a core identity to call self, we are in many ways left without a reliable story.

Postmodern storylessness can lead to a crisis in self-identity and a painful sense of lostness and despair in teens. It is imperative, then, that the church begins to address the very real issues that postmodernism can raise in our youth.

A fragmented sense of identity. Postmodern deconstruction, brought to its logical conclusion, leads to a fragmented sense of self. Who am I? A self of my own construction. This is something postmodernism both celebrates and critiques. You can finally design yourself; you can write your own story. This goes hand-in-hand with designing your own framework of truth. However, it's just your story, your own truth, so don't hold it too tightly.

Let's think about an adolescent response to the way postmodernism encourages us to design ourselves, to fashion our own framework of truth. If one's identity is created by self, there are at least three alternatives teens could likely choose. First, despair and cynicism can take root. If a sense of self-identity comes from a self that is essentially devalued or distrusted, what is the worth of that self-identity? (It doesn't help that systemic abandonment by adults, which we discussed in chapter 1, has already eroded an adolescent's sense of identity.) In an era in which there is an unashamed search for something higher, something beyond themselves—a self-constructed identity—is more than a let-down; it's suspect.

The second option is to play the game. Run with it. Have fun with the self you create, and use it to your advantage. Be the person you always wanted to be. True self-identity comes from within. But this response is more like an external application. It's like shopping for clothes. What outfit do I want to wear? What self do I want to create? This option comes very close to our culture's obsession with image. Image is about the sense of self you want to project. It's also very utilitarian. A teenager might think, "The best self-image is the one that is most useful to me. It's the one that gets me what I want and where I want to go."

The third choice would be to create a collection or montage of selves, each one useful as the situation requires. This connects with the survival ethic and a sense of abandonment. It's not uncommon for teens today, given the situation, to utilize a variety of selves. There might be the family self, the school self, the sports self, the friends self, or the youth group self. Each self follows a different ethic. But which "self" is really real? Which one is at the core of who they truly are? Teens might say it's the "self" they are with their friends. But functionally, they may pass so effortlessly between selves that it becomes difficult to really know which one is authentic.

To be fair, some of this self-definition is simply a function of growing up, of passing through the stages of adolescence in search of identity. But the fact that postmodern thinking encourages this kind of multiphrenia—the splitting of one's self into a multitude of selves—cannot be overlooked.

What's missing is the ultimate source of self. Teens are on a search for a reliable sense of self that exists at their very core. Postmodernism questions the ultimate source of one's identity. Biblically, our source of identity is God—the one who formed us and called us to be agents of God's healing in a hurting world. This stands in stark contrast to postmodern self-understanding. Postmodern identity is not connected to a fixed inner core of self; it's plastic. It's put on like layers. Much like an onion: peel away each layer and at the center there's nothing.

Adolescents tend to embrace the misguided notion that external expressions, such as style and image, ultimately define who they are. But as they mature, they begin to realize that a diffuse identity is ultimately unsatisfying. Life is lived most authentically from the inside out.

Fluid, nomadic sense of belonging. Imagine the desperation, even panic, that overcomes you when you're totally lost. Now contrast that with the feeling of safety and belonging when you're at home. In some ways this describes the adolescent sense of belonging in our postmodern context. Deconstruction argues that not only is identity a construct of self, but one's world is also a human construct. There's no true self and no real home. Any sense of belonging is fluid at best. Without a solid reality in which to feel at home, how can a young person have a clear sense of belonging? "Where do I belong? I don't know."

And to put this into the context of a fragmented identity, how can a teenager clearly answer the question of belonging if he or she doesn't have a true sense of self with which to belong? The sense of home, of belonging, and one's identity are thus clearly connected, contributing to each other.

Along with the issue of where one belongs, the question "With whom do I belong?" also confronts youth. Most teens, like the rest of us, identify with others in the same situation. They gravitate toward others who are wandering through the landscape of adolescence. They're adrift with fellow nomads in the vast wilderness of constructed reality. They're looking for home.

Obscured autonomy. As we've framed the adolescent narrative, the fundamental question of autonomy is, "Do I matter?" But with a fragmented sense of identity another question lurks, "Who is the me that matters?" "Who is the me that is being loved, that makes choices?" The fragmented identity of postmodernism haunts teens because they may have a hard time answering those questions. It's difficult for them to know which self is being valued or validated. Their sense of autonomy is hard to find; it's obscured.

Autonomy and a sense of worth are closely connected. Autonomy is self-assertion that increases as adolescents feel valued. Take Cheri, for an example. She came to college as a bright, gifted student full of potential. But she was timid, shying away from leadership opportunities. In a two-year span, I noticed her growing independence and assertiveness as she internalized her worth as a gifted leader. Her autonomy developed with her growing sense of value.

There's a sense in which adolescents need to know themselves (identity) so they can truly understand their value. This value will increase their sense of autonomy. When a young person's sense of identity is fragmented and without a center, it's very difficult to be sure if, or how, she really matters. The postmodern self obscures this sense of autonomy because there is no clear, core self to value.

Postmodernism can also call into question the value of validation. Any authentic sense of value for teens can only come from those who know them at their very core. But if there is no core self, how can there be any authentication?

Justin was on an urban mission trip in Los Angeles. One morning he shared his breakfast with a homeless man in McArthur Park. During the meal he related his story of faith. Justin's dad, also on the trip, lavishly praised him for his courage and acceptance. But what if this was only "religious" Justin on the mission trip, not the real Justin? This may have been only the self that Justin wanted his group, and his dad, to see. His father's endorsement can best guide him toward a clearer sense of identity if Justin is embracing a core "self."

Postmodernism's influence, therefore, carries a sense of anxiety for youth as they experience a fragmented sense of identity, a fluid sense of belonging, and an obscure sense of autonomy. At the same time, postmodernism presents youth and youth workers with opportunities. Postmodern thinking has reframed discussions of truth and spirituality, reminding us of Jesus' own declaration in the face of challenges to his ministry: "New wine must be put into new wineskins" (Luke 5:37-38). Those words still ring true today. While recognizing postmodernism's challenges, we must also recognize the appealing opportunities.

The Opportunities of Postmodernism

Nick, a student of mine, was in my office and we were discussing the church. We talked about our experiences with preaching we'd heard recently. Clearly frustrated at one point, Nick blurted, "I'm just so tired of all the formulas. I can't stand the sermons that promise 'three steps to a happy life,' or 'five ways to victory over sin.' Life just doesn't work that way. I want the truth. I want a whole gospel that relates to the realities of life. Not a bunch of neat and tidy principles."

Nick expressed to me one of the positive influences of postmodernism. Young people today are not interested in a glossed-over form of salvation that's been reduced to a set of principles. They want the whole Bible, warts and all. They want authenticity.

Spiritual openness. Postmodern thinking is critical of the assumptions of scientific observation and more open to ambiguities, which means more openness to the mysterious and the spiritual realm. Today, in our emerging postmodern context, spirituality is cresting. Recent studies reveal that while young people may not be active spiritual "seekers," they show great receptivity to faith.[9] Teenagers are very sympathetic to the idea of a God that is at work in their lives and in the world. The way movies such as The Matrix or books like the Harry Potter series have sparked spiritual conversations among teens is refreshing. Teens raise questions about God's existence, the ways in which God works, and how real life and current events sometimes contradict popular Christian notions of God's activity in the world.

What an open door for spiritual conversations! Youth workers have the freedom to speak from their own vantage points. For Christians, there's nothing more basic than saying the word "God" and declaring that we are redeemed by Jesus Christ. There's no need to translate our stories into neutral, modern, scientific terms. We can use God language generously as we share our own spiritual journeys.

Desire for community. Postmoderns come to church to experience a sense of spiritual family. It's a move toward a more biblical understanding of the church. The church is not a collection of individuals but a covenant community in which members are mutually accountable in matters of faith and life. Community is an essential goal of God's program for creation. God's purpose is to establish a reconciled people who enjoy fellowship with God, with one another, and ultimately with all creation. God saves us, not out of community, but for it.[10]

Preference for story. On our way through modernity we've lost the central story of Scripture. As my student Nick had observed, Scripture has been reduced to formulas and principles. But easy, pat answers are just not acceptable to postmoderns. They know that life is complicated and messy, and that a "five-step approach" isn't realistic. Postmodern students want to relate to the whole of life. They want the whole story. And the biblical story is a lot like life—often complex, painful, and puzzling.

Today's teens are tremendously open to seeing and hearing the story of faith. They want to see how their stories weave together as a community in the church, and how their stories corporately connect with the story of God. Using narrative, we can bring students to a crossroads where they can finally experience God, community, and life in an authentic way.

Relational understanding of truth. While moderns define truth propositionally, postmoderns help us rediscover the way in which truth is also relational. Jesus didn't say, "Come follow me and I'll give you propositions to be tested in a lab." Instead, he said, "I am the way . . . and the truth" (John 14:6). He offered himself and his life. Those who seek the truth are invited into a relationship with him. God sent us a person, the person of Jesus.

Conclusion

Postmodernism, with all its challenges and opportunities, provides us with a wonderful context in which the story of God can converse with the realities of today's culture. God's reign, inaugurated by Jesus, is a radical answer to both modern metanarratives of scientific power and the fragmented local narratives of postmodernism. The biblical narrative is the story of a God who created human beings in God's image, calling them to participate in the establishment of God's rule. In this new reality of God's kingdom, Christ's followers model his suffering and his self-sacrificial love. This is a narrative of compassion that doesn't lust for power but shares it. It embraces the pain of marginalized people and listens to their voice.

This is a story that captures the imagination of youth today. It offers the durable sense of identity, belonging, and autonomy for which youth are thirsting. The idea of being created and called by God is compelling to teens. As they identify with God's people and with their mission as agents of God's reign in the world, they find themselves growing in their relationship to God. They find themselves in a stable home, which they receive as a gift of God, not grasped and conquered by an autonomous self at the expense of others. Instead, they are empowered to live lives of suffering love as they follow Jesus.

In our emerging postmodern context, we have the opportunity to communicate the unchanging gospel to teens in innovative ways. The reign of God that Jesus announced is a powerful alternative to the fragmented, homeless world of postmodernism. Participating in God's reign ultimately means helping bring forth God's new reality by being the people of God in the world: belonging in true community, serving others, and inviting others to participate in God's new realm.

three

Consumerism: The New Salvation Story

My family enjoys watching the popular reality series *Extreme Makeover: Home Edition* in which new homes are built for families in need. It didn't take Shelly and me too long before we grew weary of the new homeowner's incessant use of the phrase, "Oh my God!" It was as if this was the only way to express their shock at the extravagance in which they were about to live. We grew up learning that God's people were not to "misuse the name of the Lord" (Exodus 20:7). So we winced every time we heard the phrase. Actually we got quite good at anticipating it. Each time we could sense the phrase coming we would mute the sound on the television. After awhile we felt good about our ability to keep our kids from such damage to their spiritual lives.

But after watching a few episodes—successfully muting almost all references to God—I heard something perhaps more disturbing. At the end of one show, one of my children muttered, "I wish we had a new house." At that moment I realized something was going on at a deeper level. Somehow this seemingly harmless show was sowing seeds of discontent in the minds and hearts of my children—and me.

There's a subtle but strong underlying message in a show like this. But you have to look and listen carefully. The message is, "Fulfillment comes when you have newer, bigger, and better stuff." In fact, the ad campaign promoting the show's second season featured a weeping dad thanking the design team for changing his life. "You made me a better husband, a better father, and a better man." At the close of one episode, the tearful mother asserted, "You've given me my life back." Listen to what they're saying. Doesn't it sound like a form of salvation? These are words we might expect from someone who has encountered Jesus.

In some ways the show tells us, "You can be saved from a life of insignificance and despair. When you find yourself in a struggle for happiness, dissatisfied with life and who you are, your search will ultimately lead you to a purchase." The climax of this "salvation" story comes when you finally possess the product that brings you joy. And you will live out your days with a sense of peace and inner harmony. The moral of the story is that personal acquisition is the way to fulfillment, happiness, identity, and meaning in life. But that is not all to the story. It also tells us that our identity lies in what we buy, not in what we produce. And our task is to nurture a new generation of consumers—because that's who we are.

Now, let's not be too hard on one television show. The salvation story of consumption is everywhere, and we are unwittingly manipulated to desire what our economy produces. This consuming narrative especially influences impressionable teens. Consumerism's emphasis on personal fulfillment can be closely associated with modernism, which says that human ingenuity and resourcefulness are the answer to everything. Our postmodern culture has not been able to provide the tools to overcome this materialistic orientation. As we'll see in Section Two, it is the contrast narrative of God's reign that can counter the ruse of consumerism.

So, how does consumerism shape us? How does it form our teens and nuance the contours of their story? This chapter focuses on the way our consumer culture works to create desire, and especially how it affects the adolescent narrative.

The Reality of Consumer Culture

In many ways we are formed by the narratives we receive. These stories come to us in a complex, multi-layered matrix of meaning called "culture." Our culture, which promotes a set of ideals, values, and assumptions, makes up a master plan for living and interpreting life, a map of reality.[1] It seems increasingly evident that in our society, a major component of this master plan is consumption. More and more, we're seeing a collaborative, organizational nature within culture—an industry—that is economically driven and centered on cultural products created for mass consumption.[2] Consumerism isn't limited to big business; it has extended into our cultural psyche. Consumption is being marketed as a value, emerging as a central theme in the stories of popular culture.

Its reach. Weeks before the 2006 Disney/Pixar movie *Cars* hit the big screen, its characters were already being marketed. Lightning McQueen, Sally, Mader, and Luigi were plastered all over the boxes of our favorite sugary cereals. They were marketed as Happy Meal toys. They were also part of an ad campaign for a major auto insurance company. The lovable automobiles were everywhere. There was almost no way for our family *not* to see the motion picture once it debuted. Our kids were in love with the characters before they ever experienced the movie.

But this isn't just about getting families to buy movie tickets; it's much more. It's a clever collaborative effort on the part of Disney, McDonald's, Kellogg's, and State Farm, using popular culture to leverage themselves and market their products. They sold a product while telling a powerful story: buy and be happy. This is consumerism in action.

 Our consumer culture uses the collective forces of media conglomerates, information and communications firms, and the market research giants to shape consumer desire. It accounts for the vast majority of the world's output of shared images, stories, songs, information, news, and entertainment.[3] If our individual and cultural identity is significantly shaped through shared images and stories, then consumerism has a profound effect on our personal and collective worldviews.

Consumerism's capacity to tell a consuming story and shape desire is due, in part to creativity, but primarily to its enormity. Our exposure to its mediated messages and experiences is more voluminous, more continuous, and more pervasive than ever before. Think about Rupert Murdoch's media giant News Corporation and the extent to which it reaches into so many areas of our lives. NewsCorp, as it's commonly known, owns media outlets in film, news, publishing, broadcasting, Internet, and sports. The list includes 20th Century

Fox, Fox Searchlight Pictures, Fox Television, Direct TV, the *New York Post*, the *London Times*, *TV Guide*, the Los Angeles Dodgers, the LA Lakers, the New York Rangers, the NY Knicks, Harper Collins Publishing, and Zondervan Publishers. (Zondervan, by the way, also owns youth ministry resource leader, Youth Specialties.) Imagine the influence of the collaborative effort of just one media titan. But NewsCorp is not alone. Other media mega-monsters such as AOL Time Warner, Vivendi Universal, Sony, Viacom, Walt Disney, and Bertelsmann are all competing for larger and larger amounts of brain space. They're all telling us essentially the same story: "Buy stuff and be fulfilled."

Its clout. Consumerism has been given immense power because of the notion that it's absolutely necessary to keep a capitalist, free-market economy afloat.[4] Consumption, rather than production, is driving today's brand of North American capitalism, one that's becoming increasingly global. For capitalist economies to continue chugging along, consumers must keep buying in greater and greater amounts. Consumers must therefore be convinced to buy the products that producers are creating.

Consumerism in our culture is not morally condemned as greed because it's a critically important feature of global capitalism. After the horrific World Trade Center attacks on September 11, 2001, the resounding and routine message of government officials from President Bush on down was that the most patriotic act American could perform was to go spend money.[5] Otherwise, the economy might also crumble.

The key concern in almost every corporate boardroom is, "How can we get more people to buy more of our product?" With its ability to form desires and influence consumer buying habits, consumerism has become a major player in our current economic system.

Its strategy. In a highly competitive marketplace, consumers have developed immunity to traditional corporate advertising. Companies therefore have to be about something else. The added value has become the story or idea behind the brand. Corporate brands have moved into the realm of selling pseudo-spirituality—belonging, love, community—that we used to get from other sources like family or church.[6]

The Starbucks Coffee Company understands this tactic. Taking its brand beyond the proverbial "billboard," Starbucks has created its identity by establishing strong emotional ties. It is fast being recognized as the "third place"—not home, not work. Starbucks' CEO Howard Schultz believes that people who come to Starbucks are not just there for the coffee. They come for "the romance of the coffee experience, the feeling of warmth and community that people get in Starbucks stores."[7] In an interview on the television news magazine *60 Minutes*, Schultz intimated, "We're not in the business of filling bellies. We're in the business of filling souls."[8] That sounds like another salvation story. It's more than a coffee "culture" that Starbucks is brewing.

The savvy brand builders are selling more than a product. Nike sells the essence of sport. Starbucks sells community. Coke sells love. Disney sells family and the lost, idyllic American town. Yes, these values are good, but we must ask, "To what extent do the brand builders control our collective stories? Are we going to allow the corporate brand to define and shape values such as love or community for us? Should these values be *sold to* us, or should they *come from* us?"

Our consumer culture is so pervasive and its values are so deeply ingrained that they are hard to recognize. But we must pay attention to its strategy and ability to shape our collective cultural story. We must also be sensitive to the ways in which consumerism influences the narrative of our adolescents.

Consumerism and the Adolescent Narrative

Consumerism's influence on today's teens is mammoth. Clearly, its powerful, ever-present message has affected adolescent realities of sexuality, drug use, violence, and body image. But how has it shaped their narrative in terms of identity, belonging, and autonomy?

The consumerist narrative tells teens that identity and fulfillment come through consumption and material accumulation. This idea competes with the Christian understanding that true identity and fulfillment come through our relationship with Christ as children of God. The speed and omnipresence of consumerism's media messages have increased the busyness and noise levels of today's teens. This feverish lifestyle undermines adolescent identity formation and sabotages their spiritual growth. (See the "Wide Angle" chart on page 24 for a shorthand version of this discussion).

Identity with a price tag. The over-riding narrative of consumerism is: "You are what you consume." Identity is based on what a teen can purchase and put on display. The result is that adolescent identity tends to be formed externally rather than generated internally. But how does our consumer culture tell this story? Let's take a look.

One strategy marketers use is what I'd call "identity branding." This is an explicit effort to get teens to identify themselves with a particular product or corporate brand. The craze around Apple's iPod is an example of this identity branding. As I write, the iPod is an innovative product that is changing the face of the music industry. Millions of people—many of them teens—download songs from Apple's iTunes website.[9] As a part of iPod's early and vastly successful ad campaign, the website's homepage contained a neon-colored image screaming for your attention. The image was the now familiar dark silhouette of a trendy young person passionately dancing to the music playing on the white iPod attached to his ears. The caption read, "Which iPod are you?" Notice the question wasn't "Which iPod do you prefer?" or "Which iPod suits your lifestyle?" It was an overt attempt to blend product and identity in hopes that teens would fuse their own identity with their product. With millions of consumers gobbling up iPod and iTunes products every year, the strategy of mixing identity and brand must be working.[10]

Identity branding can also incorporate personal qualities that we all idealize. Marketers anticipate that consumers will buy their products because they want to identify with and adopt those traits. For example, consider Gatorade's long-running "Is *It* in You?" ad campaign. The TV commercial spots show athletes in dark, translucent colors, driving to succeed in their sport. The sweat beading from their skin is tinted in the various colors of the latest line of the Gatorade performance drink. The images fade as the words "Is *It* in You?" emerge. Viewers are compelled to consider if "it" is in them. The way the commercial is framed associates Gatorade with more than a drink. It champions successful qualities such as desire, drive, tough-

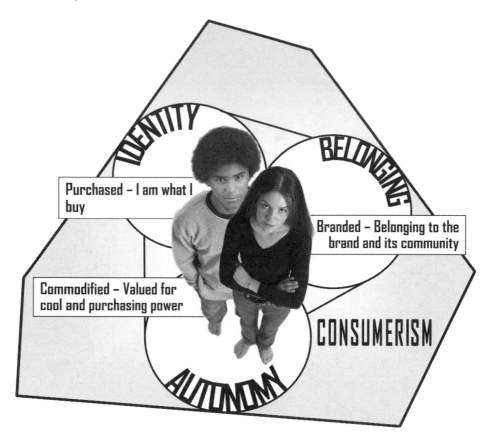

ness, perseverance, discipline, or success. In terms of identity, therefore, if a teen wishes to embody those traits, Gatorade is the drink for her. A brand has successfully formed identity.

But consumerism doesn't stop there. It also engages in a marketing strategy we could call "caricaturing." In an effort to sell their products more efficiently, corporate advertisers go so far as to design a form of adolescent identity for teens to readily adopt.

Extensive research and vast sums of marketing dollars have generated teen-targeted, media-created caricatures. One example is the "Mook." He is the crude, loud, obnoxious, in-your-face male: a teen frozen in permanent adolescence. Mooks can be found everywhere. They're the daredevils on "Jackass." They star in MTV's "Spring Break" specials. On Comedy Central, they're the cartoon cutouts of

"South Park," or the young men on the "Man Show." Other shows like "King of the Hill," "Arrested Development," and "American Dad" also exploit the Mook image. Mooks continue to be spun out as key characters in new television shows every season. You don't have to look very hard.

But there's no real Mook. It's a market creation designed to take advantage of the testosterone-driven craziness of male adolescence. Teenage males identify with it and "buy into" it. All that needs to be done is associate merchandise with the Mook caricature and you have Mooks gobbling up those products.

Along with the Mook, the media machine has also produced a female caricature. The "Midriff"—no more true to life than the Mook—is the sexually empowered, prematurely adult female. The Mook doesn't care what people think of him, but the Midriff is consumed by appearances. The Midriff is a repackaged collection of sexual clichés, but marketed as a form of empowerment. Your body is your best asset. Flaunt your sexuality even if you don't understand it.[11] Celebutantes Paris Hilton, Lindsay Lohan, and Britney Spears seem to embody the essence of the Midriff. The marketing strategy is similar to that of the Mook: project the caricature to teens and they will embrace and begin to personify it. All you need to do is infuse a brand or product into a pre-designed teen market.

Aside from marketing strategies, we must consider the relentless nature of corporate advertising. The speed of change with which consumerism brands what is cool hinders healthy identity formation. There is very little in current marketing from which a teen can find stability, constancy, and progression toward any sort of goal such as maturity. The definition of *cool* changes and the hot brands change with it. With teen identity so closely connected to brands, products, and what is "in," how can an adolescent form any kind of identity with any certainty? With the messages' rate of speed increasing and the noise of consumerism sabotaging adolescent identity formation, there is now almost no space for adolescents to slow down and reflect on life. How can young people find the time to be intentional about their identity? Even if that were possible, why would a teenager want to slow down in the first place? Our consumer culture won't allow for that option because adolescents might then become discerning individuals.

Belonging to the brand. There is a way in which we are united by what we are being sold. Almost everyone can identify the McDonald's golden arches or the Coca-Cola symbol. When it comes to the question, "How do I fit?" adolescents seem to find their sense of belonging in the brand itself. In some ways they've been branded. Corporate branding has been highly effective with teens. It's no secret that marketers desire lifelong brand loyalty; impressionable teens with vast amounts of disposable income are ready to offer their allegiance. And sure enough, teenagers show more brand loyalty than any other age group.

Take the fashion world as an example. During Nike's "Just Do It" campaign, the company broke new ground by marketing a certain lifestyle and fusing it with a brand. The promotion glorified the qualities of grit, determination, and passion. In the end, it redefined culture through sport.

As a youth pastor, I often opened youth meetings with some sort of game. Occasionally, I would have students count the number of Nike swooshes they were wearing. Winners routinely had more than thirty. Many teens wore upward of twenty. I sensed they weren't just wearing fashionable clothes. They were loyally displaying a lifestyle they internalized, buying the dream Nike sold them.

More recently, Abercrombie and Fitch has been a leading retailer among teens. The Abercrombie and Fitch image is of party-loving, athletic males and scantily clad women living fantasy lives. The company positions itself as offering the highest quality, casual, All-American lifestyle clothing for aspirational men and women. At least in the United States, what American adolescent doesn't want to live the "All-American" life? What teenager doesn't want to aspire to the good life? The corporate message has taken hold. By endorsing the Abercrombie and Fitch name in droves, teens are doing more than personifying a lifestyle; they're being loyal to the brand that champions it. This isn't to say that *all* teens are brand loyalists. Some savvy and thoughtful adolescents, influenced by some sort of counternarrative (Christian or other), are aware of these brand-influence strategies. But sadly, the vast majority of teens have been swayed by brand appeal.

Adolescents also sense that they belong in the "brand community." Companies are very effective at building such communities on product websites. Mountain Dew targets mostly young, on-the-edge, free-spirited, extreme consumers. When I checked out its website I could download "dew music" or click on various tabs for MDTV, gaming, promos, brands, and downloads. I quickly discovered that the website is not about disseminating nutritional facts about various soft drink products. It's about creating and strengthening a sense of community. I clicked the "join dew" tab. There I could register, update my profile, and be a part of the Mountain Dew community. The motto there is telling: "You're on the path to be one of the few— the proud—the green."[12]

I remember speaking at a Christian camp for high school students. I presented pairs of word pictures (such as "river or lake," "SUV or convertible") and asked campers to select which word picture best described who they were. One of the word pairs was "Sprite or Mountain Dew." In unison, with fist-bumps, high-fives enveloped in a deafening cheer, almost the entire camp screamed for Mountain Dew. In this roar of solidarity they affirmed to each other that they were part of the "Dew" community.

For teens, brand loyalty is not really about consuming products such as Mountain Dew or iPods. It's more about the bond and the connectedness they sense within the brand community. Consumerism has successfully nurtured a sense of belonging.

Commodified autonomy. How does our consumer culture demonstrate to teens that they matter? Corporate brands send a very powerful message to teens: they are valued for their spending power and for their claim on "cool." There are two areas in which this message is conveyed: consumer influence, and image and style.

First, adolescent autonomy comes with their consumer influence. The corporate market machine values them for their ability to spend vast amounts of money. With wads of cash, teens are flexing their economic muscle and marketers are salivating over this massive consumer group. According to the Mintel International Group, a leading supplier of consumer intelligence, teen spending in the United States was projected to be $190 billion in 2006. In addition, these twelve-to seventeen-year-olds would convince their parents to spend an estimated $128.5 billion. That means teens will influence the expenditure of more than $318 billion in 2006. That figure, which surpasses the gross domestic product of many countries, represents a lot of spending power. And the trend is that those numbers will continue to rise.

Since the late 1990s, teenagers have become the most marketed-to segment of the North American population. With the financial bottom line always in mind, consumerism conglomerates such as Viacom, Universal/Vivendi, and others have invested vast sums of money and creative energy in the market research of the teenage population. The real concern is to find a way to get teens' money. Most teens don't sense it immediately, but eventually they can become wary of corporate consumeristic intentions. They see it as a sort of colonization of their lives: influencing teens' minds and hearts, gaining loyalty in order to access their resources.

In response, companies have become quite sophisticated and cunning. For example, in the 1990s, Sprite, a company struggling to keep pace in the ultra-competitive soft drink market, began poking fun at their own ads. Then it launched a marketing campaign in which the company cloaked itself in hip-hop cool. With the cooperation of media icon MTV, Sprite moved into the heart of teen culture.[13] Sprite not only gained unprecedented access to the adolescent world; it became a part of the teen hip-hop culture itself. Sprite and urban authenticity became synonymous.

Who is validating our teens today? Consumerism has swooped in and is selling the story that teens matter to the corporate branders. And why do they matter? Not because they are loved in a virtuous or altruistic sense. They matter because of their money, because they have the power to spend. Consumerism sees adolescents' value and their power to choose as nothing more than a commodity. Teenage autonomy is based on a shallow, callous, pragmatic sense of value.

Second, adolescent autonomy has to do with image and style. A lucrative strategy for corporate brands is to capture and sell "cool." "Cool hunting" is a relatively recent paradigm in market research.[14] It's not structured around the whims of Madison Avenue, where the money is, but around values and expressions of a given player in a social network. Corporate cool hunters are searching for teens that have the respect, trust, and admiration of their friends. They're looking for cool. Embedded in teen culture, these sleeper agents extract "coolness" from those who exude cool, and broker it to those who don't. Marketing firms such as Look-Look and the Zandl Group interpret and "forecast" their findings on their corporate websites, giving companies exclusive access to cool for an immense premium.

The direct and instant access of cool hunting has created something of a feedback loop. Consumerism captures the latest trends in youth image and style, brings it to market, and sells it back to teens. Teenagers consume it and project it back, embodying the cool they already embrace. In a very real sense, consumerism has become the lens through which adolescents see themselves, and they want to emulate what they see. Ironically, cool hunting kills what it finds. Once cool is brought to market it's been exposed and made available to the masses. So, cool moves onto the next thing or drives further underground. The faster and more efficient the feedback loop works, the harder cool is to find.

The feedback loop created by consumerism's search for cool has an implicit, but clearly understood message: image and style are valued over substance. Adolescents themselves are obsessed enough with facade and veneer. Now the forces of consumerism are reinforcing that myth with power and precision. A teenager might wonder, "What about me matters most?" The answer is not strong character or deep integrity. The deafening answer is image and style. The answer is cool. And this loop has become so powerful that it effectively drives off other forms of influence. Parental and religious influences wishing to cultivate deeper values and character traits like compassion, generosity, or service must be creative and intentional if they hope to compete. Perhaps the most effective strategy is to tell and retell the story of God's reign as a contrast narrative that challenges the assumptions of consumerism.

Conclusion

Consumer culture powerfully influences our teenagers. Among our culture's arsenal of messages, perhaps its most destructive weapon is the salvation story of consumption. Entertainment conglomerates and communications giants have joined forces to form the desire to consume.

Most adolescents believe that their identity and fulfillment come through consumption, not by knowing and following Jesus in life. Belonging is found in the brand and its community. A sense of autonomy emerges from their power to spend and their ability to capture and broker the latest in cool. My experience leads me to believe that most Christian adolescents buy this story too. But in the face of consumerism's pervasive influence, we can offer a contrasting story. The counternarrative of God's reign can rescript the idea of "the good life." It can also reconnect their sense of identity and fulfillment in Christ, and help them discover a sense of belonging with the faith community.

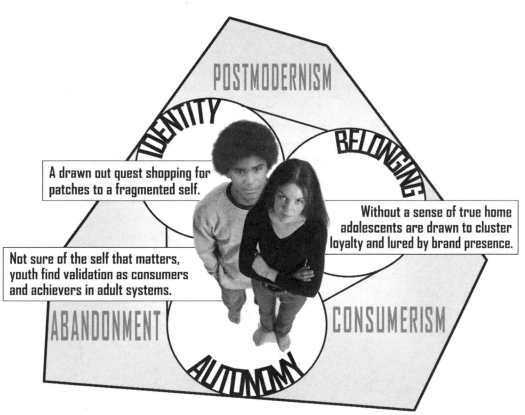

POSTMODERNISM

IDENTITY

BELONGING

A drawn out quest shopping for patches to a fragmented self.

Without a sense of true home adolescents are drawn to cluster loyalty and lured by brand presence.

Not sure of the self that matters, youth find validation as consumers and achievers in adult systems.

ABANDONMENT

CONSUMERISM

AUTONOMY

Before We Move On

We've been framing the adolescent narrative with the three primary questions of individuation, "Who am I?" "How do I fit?" and "Do I really matter?" It is therefore important to briefly review the contemporary adolescent narrative around the framework of identity, belonging, and autonomy.

Identity. Our culture of abandonment has protracted the adolescent quest for identity. Without a significant adult presence, identity is hard enough to find, much less form. Postmodern deconstruction has fragmented teens' sense of identity. One's identity has been de-centered; it's nothing more than a self-made construct. Consumerism has led young people to believe their identity can be purchased. "You are what you consume."

Belonging. In the context of abandonment, the belonging is most palpable in the peer cluster. The seemingly hostile adult world has driven adolescents underground where they feel they belong: in their own world. Postmodern thinking leads to a nomadic sense of belonging. There's no true self and no fixed reality; there's no home. Our consumer-driven culture has branded our teens. They not only wear the brand, they belong to the brand and its community.

Autonomy. In a culture marked by abandonment, adolescents might get the feeling that they are valued only for the ways they contribute to the pursuits of the adults around them, not for the unique creations that they are. The postmodern de-centered self can make it very difficult for adolescents to be sure if, or how, they really matter. And consumer culture has commodified adolescents' sense of autonomy. Teens are valued as brokers of cool and for their cash.

THE COUNTERNARRATIVE OF GOD'S REIGN

WIDE ANGLE

Framework	The Kingdom Counternarrative			
Individuation	Story Dimension	Connecting Dimension	Transforming Dimension	Future-Now Dimension
Identity	Rooted in God's bigger story	Formed in context of community	Solidified as change agents	Defined and durable
Belonging	Connected to God's people	Affirmed in the faith family	Clarified as a contrast culture	Expressed in a contrast vision
Autonomy	Authenticated in God's mission	Confirmed as fellow-travelers	Developed as participants in God's call	Strengthened by a sense of purpose

four

The Reign of God

A few years ago, the students in my Discipleship and Evangelism class spent time in Wichita, Kansas, working with the urban ministry, World Impact. We were invited for lunch at Carson Middle School. Over the years, the school had become increasingly violent. Students who weren't involved in gangs were intimidated by them, and rising hostility made the lunchroom a dangerous battle zone.

We were there at the invitation of the school's assistant principal, who was determined to curb the escalating violence. He asked us to hang out with the students, build relationships, and have a good time. With our decks of cards, table games, and crafts, we must have looked like the fun patrol.

An armed officer guarded the door. This lunchroom "monitor," a retired 15-year police veteran, briefed us on how lunch "went down": Girls and boys would eat in separate rooms, in three shifts of twenty minutes each.

I wasn't prepared for what came next. The moment the middle-schoolers entered the room, the attitude of the authorities and the atmosphere radically changed. The monitor became a drill sergeant at boot camp. Anyone who stepped out of line, or subverted the system in any way, felt the wrath of this intimidator. It was an in-your-face, belittling, insulting tirade, with predictions of future prison time.

I was appalled. My students were terrified. But the boys at the school didn't even flinch; it was business as usual. This place was operating under a culture of terror. Fear and intimidation were the only effective tools for controlling behavior. But imagine how ill-prepared and unnerved we were.

Still, we naively went ahead with our plan. With two college students per table, we began with some small talk and a fun game. To our surprise the boys slowly warmed up to us. Before too long, they were laughing and high-fiving each other. There were even a few chest bumps. At the end, the boys gathered around tables, watching magic tricks with a giddy innocence lost long ago. Some of my students even exchanged email addresses with boys, promising to stay connected.

When the lunch period was over, our boot-camp intimidator gathered us together. With tears in his eyes, he said, "In all my years of doing this, I've never seen this lunchroom transformed like it was today. I thought this would never happen."

What happened that day in a middle school lunch room was a kingdom sighting. The reign of God had broken into a world of fear. The genuine love and compassion of our students not only attracted these normally hardened boys; it altered the culture. The episode illustrated the transforming nature of God's reign. A contrast culture surfaced and the old order was exposed. A new way of living was revealed. The dominant culture was affected, and others were invited to participate in the emerging reality.

The Reign of God as a Foundation for Youth Ministry

I believe the reign of God offers teens a compelling counternarrative to the story written for them by our current culture.[1] As a counternarrative, its power is rooted in the fact that God's reign is a deeply biblical paradigm. By paradigm I mean that it is a compelling, transcendent archetype from which principles, strategies, and practices are derived. It functions as a theoretical framework, or a set of assumptions, that makes up a way of viewing reality.

As a biblical paradigm God's reign represents an overarching biblical theme. It brings a level of coherence and clarity to the biblical story, God's activity in the world, and God's relationship with humanity. It provides a framework for a biblical way of viewing life, faith, and the world. Because the kingdom of God is a biblical paradigm, it ought to operate as a pattern for youth ministry.

Youth ministry based merely on theological *principles* truncates the gospel and has run its course. As a *paradigm*, however, God's reign offers a theologically faithful foundation for youth ministry in the twenty-first century. By embracing it, we also embrace a kingdom-driven theology of the church as a whole, thus helping us understand how youth ministry fits into the broader identity and mission of the church as an agent of God's reign. What follows is an introduction to the kingdom of God and a discussion of its various dimensions as a biblical paradigm.

The Reign of God in Scripture[2]

God's reign has its roots in the Old Testament. After the rampaging Egyptian army had been vanquished at the Red Sea, Moses and Miriam led the Israelites in a victory hymn. The song declares "The LORD will reign for ever and ever" (Exodus 15:18). As an infant nation, Israel was ruled by Yahweh. When the Israelites wanted to be like other nations with human rulers, they rejected God as king (1 Samuel 8:7).

Those living under Yahweh's reign were to embody kingdom values such as equality, justice, and righteousness. But guided by human kings, the people of God moved away from God's kingdom purposes. The prophets continually reminded the kings and the people of God's ultimate reign and called them back to its priorities (Isaiah 40-55; Amos 3-6; Micah 6-7).

In its worship, the people of Israel declare that God's reign will never end. God upholds the oppressed and cares for the marginalized, and ultimately God will be exalted among the nations of the earth (Psalms 9, 146, and 46).

In the New Testament, Paul identifies God's kingdom as one of "righteousness, peace and joy in the Holy Spirit" (Romans 14:17). In God's mercy and grace, believers have been rescued from the dominion of darkness and have been brought into the "kingdom of the Son he loves" (Colossians 1:12-13). Those who are poor in the eyes of the world will inherit the kingdom (James 2:5). And followers growing in Christ-like qualities will receive a rich welcome into the eternal kingdom of our Lord (2 Peter 1:5-11). God's ultimate vision is that one day the kingdom of this world will become "the kingdom of our

Lord and of its Messiah, and he will reign forever and ever" (Revelation 11:15).

Jesus and God's Reign

The reality of a people called by God and living under God's rule can be seen throughout the Scriptures. However, God's reign is most visible in the teaching of Jesus. The kingdom of God was at the core of Jesus' ministry.[3] Jesus announced the good news of God's kingdom, urged his followers to give it top priority, and taught his disciples to pray for God's reign to come (Mark 1:14; Matthew 6:10, 33; Luke 11:2). In Jesus' future vision, God's kingdom was pivotal. When asked about the end of the age, Jesus answered, "This good news of the kingdom will be proclaimed throughout the world, as a testimony to all the nations; and then the end will come" (Matthew 24:14).

What is God's reign? The kingdom of God might best be defined as "the dynamic rule or reign of God."[4] It's a new order under God. It is *both* a future unfolding *and* a present reality. With Jesus' arrival, the kingdom began to unfold. Jesus both embodied and announced a new realm. He summoned others to join the remaking of God's people and their new direction.[5] Jesus inaugurated God's reign, even if its ultimate consummation was still to come.

The gospel and the kingdom. The reign of God and the gospel are closely related. Jesus called for repentance and belief in the "good news" (Mark 1:15), the "gospel" of Jesus Christ. Jesus is both the content and the author of that gospel.[6] Mark depicts the good news as "the gospel of the kingdom" (Mark 4:23; 9:35)—that in Jesus the kingdom is here, and yet it continues and spreads under the reign of the risen and glorified Lord. Jesus embodied the gospel of the kingdom that he proclaimed. So, believing *in* Jesus Christ also means believing what Jesus Christ taught about the reign of God.[7]

The political nature of God's reign. The kingdom of God moves beyond the inward and spiritual dimension to affect every facet of life. It has concrete social and political dimensions. Jesus understood that he was conducting his ministry in a politically charged context.[8] Under the thumb of Rome, most Jews wanted liberation.[9] Their memory of the exodus stirred hopes of a coming new kingdom. Jesus' announcement that a radical and new realm had arrived, therefore, posed a threat to the Romans and to the Jewish religious elite.

Jesus began his ministry with a struggle against three alternative kingdoms while being tempted in the wilderness. The struggle against prevailing social institutions was symbolized by the mountain (political), the temple (religious), and the bread (economic).[10]

Jesus openly criticized kings and rulers, calling Herod a fox (Mark 10:42; Luke 13:32). Mocking Jesus as the "king of the Jews" (Luke 23:38), the Romans had him crucified, a form of execution for those found guilty of opposing the state.[11] On the religious front, Jesus regularly defied Sabbath laws and provoked the Pharisees (Matthew 12:1-14; Mark 2:23-3:6; Luke 13:10-17; John 5:2-18; Matthew 23). All four Gospels record Jesus' purging of the temple (Matthew 21:12-13; Mark 11:15-19; Luke 19:45-48; John 2:13-17); in this decisive act, Jesus struck at the nerve center of Jewish religion, challenging religious structures and signaling that the new kingdom welcomed all (Luke 4:23-27).

In poverty-riddled Palestine, Jesus preached against economic injustice (Luke 6:20, 24). In his encounter with the rich young ruler, Jesus revealed that wealth was a barrier to entering the kingdom (Luke 18:18-30). In his meeting with Zacchaeus, Jesus announced that emptying ones bank account by giving to the poor was a sign that salvation had come (Luke 19:1-10). Jesus' Jubilee proclamation was a vision that would, in effect, upset the social order (Luke 4:18-19). Land would be redistributed, slaves would be set free, and debts would be erased.

Two worlds in tension. The reign Jesus inaugurated, therefore, was not apolitical. It was simply at odds with "the kingdom of this world." Jesus declared, "My kingdom is not from this world" (John 18:36) and lived what seemed to be an inverted way of life, in stark contrast to the prevailing social system. Most notably, Jesus focused his ministry on the marginalized and oppressed. He identified with outcasts, tax collectors, and "sinners." In his patriarchal society, he elevated the status of women (Matthew 5:3-6; 9:10-12; John 4:1-42; Luke 8:1-3). Jesus called adults to become like little children. He taught that the last will be first. And he declared that greatness is attained in service (Matthew 18:3-5; 19:30; Mark 10:43). Jesus challenged his followers to love their enemies and resist evil non-violently (Matthew 5:38-48; Luke 6:32-34). He proclaimed a kingdom that challenged the pattern of society.

While God's realm and "the world" are in tension, however, Jesus never advocated for an isolated kingdom. It is not geographically or socially separate from the world. Kingdom-seekers model a contrast lifestyle and culture that run counter to that of the world, but are within that same world. Jesus' ministry exemplified engagement with the world (Mark 2:13-17; Luke 7:36-50). Participants in God's reign do not isolate themselves from the larger society; in fact, they invite others to join a community that accomplishes God's purposes in the world.

Allegiance and identity. A biblical understanding of God's reign raises some significant questions. To what kingdom do I belong? With whom do I identify? Jesus' call was to "strive first for the kingdom of God and his righteousness" (Matthew 6:33). He also declared, "Give therefore to the emperor the things that are the emperor's, and to God the things that are God's" (Matthew 22:21). Recognizing God's authority means we give God our primary allegiance. All other loyalties are placed at a secondary level.[12] We must be clear about where our loyalties lie and be prepared to make some hard choices where the strategies and goals of earthly kingdoms run counter to God's reign.

The very term *kingdom* implies a realm occupied by citizens. The kingdom of God is a collective of interdependent people who have surrendered their hearts and relationships to God's reign. Yes, individuals do make choices about kingdoms, but participating in God's reign means being grafted into a new community within the larger society. Together, believers form a people living under Christ's headship as members of his kingdom.[13] Membership in this kingdom defines our relationship to Christ, to other citizens, and to other realms. Kingdom-seekers identify themselves with a new order. They know the intimacy of community will carry them through life, and the synergy of community will increase their influence in the world.

The Church and the Kingdom

How is the church a part of God's reign? While the church is not the kingdom, as a sign of God's reign in the world it engages society. Christ launched the reality of the kingdom into the world, and God's people are witnesses of this new order.

The church's mission must hold to the reign of God as its compass. The essence of the Great Commission is a call for the church to carry God's kingdom agenda around the globe. As a part of "making disciples," the church must dethrone idols, free people from demonic powers and oppression, heal the sick, and invite people into a saving relationship with God through Christ.[14] For Jesus, the gospel was the announcement that the reign of God had arrived. Now, the church draws back the curtain of the coming kingdom, unveiling the horizon of the world's future.[15]

The church's *mission* is to be God's people who are both called and sent to represent God's reign. The church's *vocation* is to represent God's reign as its *people*, revealing a new humanity that lives in genuine community. God's authority is embodied in the new pattern of our involvement in the world. With compassion and justice, the people of God can bring wholeness and dignity to the world. And when it does, the church provides a taste of God's present and coming reign. As the church announces the kingdom's presence and authority, the world sees and touches God's reign; God's rule becomes tangible.[16] When we pray, "your kingdom come, your will be done on earth as it is in heaven," we participate in the reality of God's reign now. We do this knowing God's reign will be fulfilled when Christ returns.[17]

Contemporary Christians tend to reduce the reign of God into simplified categories, diminishing its influence on their lives. Is the kingdom spiritual or social? Is it future or present? Is it individual or corporate, personal or political, earthly or heavenly? God's reign is all of the above. To be the church, sent and called to represent God's reign, we must hold these categories in tension rather than separating them. The church is called to be a place "clearly visible to the world, in which people are faithful to their promises, love their enemies, tell the truth, honor the poor, suffer for righteousness, and thereby testify to the amazing community-creating power of God."[18]

Youth Ministry and the Reign-of-God Paradigm

As we have seen, God's reign is a theme woven through the entire biblical narrative. It captures both the depth and breadth of the gospel and the complexities of life. The paradigm of God's reign integrates various essential dimensions. Since it captures the bigger narrative of how God works in the world, the reign of God has a *story* dimension. Since it is a collective social reality in which God's people interact, it also has a *connecting* dimension. The reign of God also carries a *transformational* dimension in that God's mission is to use us to transform our broken and dying world. Finally, the kingdom has an *eschatological* dimension because, through the church, it unveils God's vision for the future.

Integrating kingdom dimensions can give youth ministries a foundation that is theologically faithful, contextually dynamic, and practically effective. As the following diagrams and commentaries show, each of these dimensions has tension points that reflect the dynamic nature and mystery of God's reign.[19] Understanding God's reign means recognizing these tensions and living within them.

A story dimension. The reign of God both captures the biblical narrative and offers us a narrative by which we can live today. In that way the kingdom of God incorporates a story dimension that is twofold. These parallel tensions are, on one spectrum: *storylessness* and *God's story*, and on the other: *one's personal story* and *the story of God's people* (see figure 1, page 83). A theology of God's reign can move young people from a sense of storylessness to embracing the story of God. God's kingdom can also help teens intersect their personal and communal narratives with the stories of the Old Testament people of God, the New Testament church, the church throughout history, and the contemporary people of God around the world. It weaves the teens' own narratives together with God's covenantal relationship with God's people, the call of the prophets, the ministry of Jesus, the teaching of the apostles, and God's future vision for his people.

The gospel of the kingdom is one in which Christians tell the story of Jesus' life, death, and resurrection. It is a story of God's mission to bless the world through a people and to reconcile the world to God.

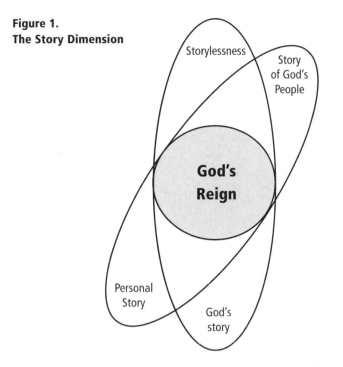

Figure 1.
The Story Dimension

Storylessness

Story
of God's
People

God's
Reign

Personal
Story

God's
story

As we tell the narrative of God's reign, we find ourselves entering into the unfolding event of the story, inviting others to participate in the drama. As we retell the story of God's kingdom, we are compelled to communicate it in fresh, innovative ways for changing contexts. And as we reconnect to the roots of the gospel narrative, we discover how the story both shapes us at our core, and influences the world. In many ways, God's reign isn't really a story we chose, but a narrative that chose us.[20]

Today's adolescents have had their stories fragmented by postmodernity. Paradoxically, they've absorbed the story of personal consumption produced by our consumer culture. Churches and youth ministries that take seriously the reign of God as a paradigm for ministry must also take seriously the fabric of the gospel narrative. This means retelling the story of God's relationship with his people throughout Scripture and history. It means telling the contemporary stories of God's people around the world. God has been, is, and will be forming a people whom he will bless and through whom God will bless the world. As contemporary Christians, we have the amazing opportunity to participate in that story.

A connecting dimension. God's reign integrates a dimension that is relational in character. Understanding the nature of God's kingdom and one's place within it helps define and develop a young person's relationship with God and with others in the faith community. The tension in the kingdom's relational dimension is *individual* and *communal* (see figure 2). There is a level in which we all enter the kingdom through an individual decision. Our faith is expressed in personal change. But the kingdom is also about community. It's important

Figure 2.
The Connecting Dimension

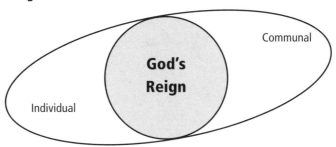

to understand community as the context of our faith. We live out our faith in relationships. A kingdom theology, therefore, can help teens understand that they are *individuals within community*. Their faith is expressed both personally and corporately.

It is in the connecting dimension where our typical, privatized understanding of discipleship and evangelism is challenged. Discipleship can best be described as "following Jesus" (Mark 8:34). In the Beatitudes, however, the marks of disciples are not primarily individualistic character traits. For example, how can a person hunger and thirst for justice (Matthew 5:6), show mercy (v. 7), or work for peace (v. 9) in a private and personal way? The Beatitudes paint a picture of a disciple community "performing" the gospel as a community rooting its life in the promise of God's kingdom.[21] These discipleship markers can't really be demonstrated in a way other than in the context of community. Embodying and performing this new ethic requires a supportive and encouraging corporate life. The gospel is most fully experienced in the setting of community.

Our consumer culture's emphasis on self-fulfillment, the postmodern notion the gospel as a form of therapy, and the personal piety of evangelicalism have squeezed today's teens into the mold of individualism. For a youth ministry to embrace a kingdom-driven paradigm, this relational dimension must be taken seriously. Kingdom-driven youth ministries can rediscover the communal nature of the faith experience. They can help young people embrace the richness of the faith community, a living lab for the faith journey. For today's teens who are predisposed to community, this is a wonderful opportunity.

A transforming dimension. The reign of God also is transformational because it calls people and society to an alternative culture that is different from the surrounding world. The polarity of the kingdom's transforming dimension is *personal* and *societal* (see figure 3). Entering the kingdom means personal change on many fronts (Mark 1:15). Deepening levels of personal change, however, lead to commitment to societal transformation (Luke 1:51-53; 3:4-6). The reign of God, as a guiding paradigm for youth ministry, can move teens through personal change to integrating societal transformation as an expression of their faith. In a dynamic way, the church, as a people, is a communal change agent. It can move teens through the contours of personal change into the realm of a communal faith experience. Then, in the context of community, individuals in the church seek to transform the societal landscape.

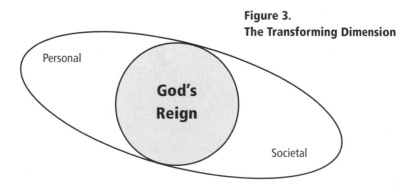

**Figure 3.
The Transforming Dimension**

Personal

God's
Reign

Societal

As we see ourselves and our youth ministries in the context of God's kingdom, we are invited to consider the ways we engage our prevailing culture. What does it mean to be the church in our contemporary context? How do we participate with God to impact our culture and our world? Along with the broader aspects of discipleship and evangelism, this is where we wrestle with our ecclesiology: How are we to be the church?

Although it is not associated with any particular human regime, God's reign is a realm and we have the opportunity to *enter* it (Matthew 5:20; 7:21; Mark 9:47; 10:25; Luke 18:24-25; John 3:5; Acts 14:22). This moves the church to consider "an invitation of companionship."[22] God, who reigns in love, intends to bless the whole earth. This God has extended an invitation for all humanity to receive the gift of God's reign in their lives. For those who have accepted the invitation, the faith community becomes a companion for them as fellow travelers.

In a world in which teens grapple with a sense of abandonment and the pursuit of purchased fulfillment, the kingdom of God stands as a compelling alternative. With this in mind, youth ministries can see their witness more as "modeling" and "inviting" than "winning" or "selling." As individual Christians, and as a faith community, the church is called to model the radical alternative of God's reign, and to winsomely invite others to enter that realm and participate in its reality.

A future-now dimension. God's kingdom also embodies an eschatological dimension as it models God's preferred future now. The tension in this dimension of God's reign is that it is both *present* and *future* (see figure 4, page 87). The kingdom of God is a present reality lived and expressed in the now. However, the present expression of God's reign points to the future culmination of the kingdom. The watching world is able to see the future rule of God now breaking in among God's people. A youth ministry guided by God's reign can move students from clinging to a private spirituality to expressing their faith publicly in the context of community, giving others a window through which they see the future reign of God.

This means youth ministries must consider the implications of

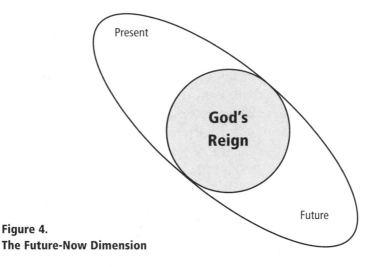

Figure 4.
The Future-Now Dimension

modeling a new and alternative culture before a watching world. Participating in God's reign means embracing the idea that a faith community—including its youth ministry—can be a sign of God's coming new order, a world in which God reigns. Perhaps it's in this dimension that the liberating good news of the gospel becomes most tangible (Isaiah 61:1-2; Matthew 11:4-6; Luke 4:18-19). This is where biblical concepts of justice, compassion, service, and self-sacrifice rise to the surface.

These ideas, however, should be understood within the framework of the other kingdom dimensions. What, for example, does it mean to participate in compassionate, selfless social justice as an individual disciple of Jesus who lives within the context of a faith community? And how does my faith community understand its mission and identity as a witness to God's purposes in the world?

The future-now dimension of God's reign emphasizes the "already but not yet." God's kingdom has *already* arrived, but is *not yet* fully here. This is where the church comes in. The faith community embodies and announces an alternative identity and vision that is already here and yet still to come. The church is "first fruits," the beginning of what's coming. The church communicates to the world what God plans to do because it shows that God is already doing it.[23]

Conclusion

As each dimension of God's reign is integrated, more gospel and faith concepts are woven into the fabric of a youth ministry and its strategies. This integration not only adds theological depth and breadth, but also makes youth ministry more durable and effective. Figure 5 depicts the multiple dimensions of God's reign, its direction, and its invitation to the world. God's reign embodies an alternative realm and vision. Those who have already received God's present and future reign invite others to enter it. God's kingdom people embrace their counternarrative as God's story of compassion and mercy for the world. They follow Jesus by living out a contrast ethic in the context of authentic community.

The theme of a people called by God and living under the rule of God is seen throughout Scripture. At the core of Jesus' mission and message was the good news of the kingdom of God. Jesus embodied the gospel of the kingdom that he proclaimed. Believing in Jesus Christ means we believe him about the reign of God.

Figure 5. The Dimensions of God's Reign

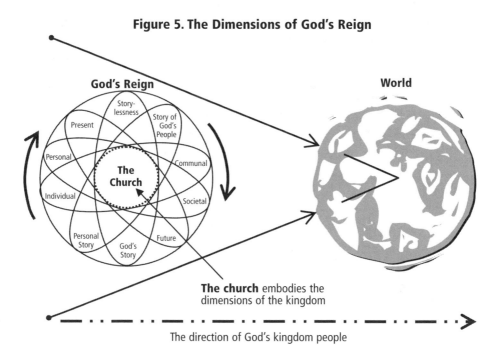

The **church** embodies the dimensions of the kingdom

The direction of God's kingdom people

The kingdom that Jesus announced is not just an inward and personal state of being; it is a social reality that was in contrast to the prevailing order of things. The church is not the kingdom. It gathers around the center of Jesus Christ and his kingdom call, holding the various dimensions of God's reign in tension. Jesus' kingdom vision is what unifies and drives the church in its interaction with the world. The church is called and sent by God to represent God's reign, announcing God's presence and authority. By living out the gospel of the kingdom, the church participates in God's greater mission to the world.

The reign of God is a paradigm that can form a firm foundation for contemporary youth ministry. Unlike a set of principles, it is multi-dimensional. The dynamic dimensions of the kingdom point to its effectiveness in today's world. As a narrative of compassion, the reign of God addresses the postmodern deconstruction of violent and conquering metanarratives. As a community, it touches the longings of today's teens that have been abandoned by adult systems. As a contrast culture, it counters the salvation narrative of consumer culture by pointing to a new and liberating realm of generosity, compassion, and celebration. Like the culture of compassion and joy shown in that middle school lunch room, the gospel of the kingdom unveils a competing and attractive reality—and it really is good news.

The Kingdom Narrative in Four Dimensions

90

five

The Reign of God as a Counternarrative

Every once in a while, when my children face the challenges of telling the truth, I tell them one of my favorite stories, an Asian folktale called "The Emperor's Seeds." An aging emperor in search of a worthy successor gave a seed to every child in the realm, asking them to plant it at home. A year later, the emperor would judge their plants to determine the next ruler of the empire.

The children all anxiously waited for their seeds to sprout. After some time, they began boasting of their flourishing, flowering plants. But the plant of a boy named Ling did not grow. Even though he watered it faithfully, his was only a pot of dirt.

When the long-awaited day came for the children to bring their plants to the palace, Ling wanted to stay home. His mother urged him to take his well-watered pot of dirt anyway. As the children gathered in the courtyard, Ling felt sick to his stomach. All the other children had lush, colorful plants; his was just an empty pot. He cowered in the corner as the others laughed at him and his pile of dirt.

"Today I will announce the next emperor!" proclaimed the monarch. His palace guards were sent among the children and their sprawling plants. They cornered Ling and his pot of nothing. As Ling was brought to the front, the courtyard fell silent. Ling thought he was being singled out as . . . a laughing stock.

The emperor, however, looked at Ling. "What is your name?" he asked. Ling was afraid to raise his head. "My name is Ling" he said sheepishly.

"Behold your new emperor!" the king announced. "His name is Ling!"

No one could believe it. How could Ling be the new emperor?

"One year ago," the emperor said. "I gave each of you a special seed. They were all boiled so they would not grow. Only Ling had the honesty and the courage to bring me a pot with my seed in it. Therefore he is your next emperor."

I use the story of Ling as a counternarrative to the story my children hear all too often in their world. "Lie. Fib. Fudge a little. It works." I could just say, "Tell the truth." But a story like this one places truth-telling and honesty in the context of life. In a way, it models honesty much more powerfully than any lecture could. There is power in stories. They teach us as they draw us in. We experience them. We identify with the plot and the characters. And if a story is compelling enough, it begins to "rescript" our own narrative.

In this book, we have spent a lot of time focusing on the contemporary adolescent narrative: how influential forces shape the way they answer questions of identity, belonging, and autonomy. In chapter 4 we explored the biblical paradigm of the reign of God as a guiding theme for youth ministry. Now we'll dive further into theology, exploring the contours of God's reign as a compelling counternarrative.

Theological work is important in youth ministry. Young people take their theology seriously, trafficking in it every single day.[1] But for the most part they're not aware of it because culture impresses myriad theologies on their souls—some competing, some even contradictory. Adolescent theology often proves to be false, incomplete, inadequate, or inconsistent. To be effective in ministry, youth workers today must come to grips with their own theology and then be able to contextualize it for their teens. Unfortunately, however, too many of us involved in the spiritual nurture of young people are not only inadequately aware of our own theology, but also unclear about the forces that shape adolescent theology.

In this chapter, therefore, let us explore the reign of God as a theology—a story that counters the theologies that influence the adolescent narrative.

A Narrative That Is Right for Our Time

A youth ministry that embraces God's reign as a guiding paradigm can meet the needs of contemporary teens. It can engage the blaring narrative of their culture by creating a competing, contrasting reality in the context of community. Within the framework of authentic relationship and community, a radically different narrative of God's realm can be told. What follows are ways in which God's reign functions as a counternarrative.

A culture of presence in a world of abandonment. It is clear that contemporary teens are in great need of a safe place in which they strongly get a sense of community and belonging. In what ways does the paradigm of God's reign counter the systemic absence of adults in the lives of teens? In God's reign, there is no place for abandonment. It's a reality of incarnated presence. Adults in the church have the tremendous opportunity to "live among" their young people, assisting them on the path toward adulthood. The entire faith community has the opportunity to welcome its teens, opening its arms of blessing.

In the kingdom, the needs of others become primary. The call to the church is to bear with the youth and carry their burdens (Colossians 3:13; Galatians 6:2). Today's teens are becoming increasingly marginalized, suffering at the hands of self-focused adults and competing adult systems. Jesus taught that the marginalized and oppressed were at the center of his kingdom (Matthew 5:3; 11:5; Luke 4:18) and that true greatness comes by serving them (Matthew 2:26-27; John 13). A primary venue for this ministry of healing is among youth.

The church has the unprecedented opportunity to be the good news of the kingdom by being present to their teens. That means we develop compassion for their adolescent journey. We hear their stories, and we . . . listen. We can involve teens at all levels of congregational life. And most importantly, we can infuse our youth ministries with more adults and a wider variety of them.

Firm reality in a fluid world. The postmodern tidal wave has created a sea of change. The postmodern narrative tells teens that nothing can be completely trusted: not reality, not truth, not self. As a result, their identities have been atomized; they feel they must borrow "selves" from a variety of influences, creating a "'patchwork self' . . . [that is] an extremely fragile—and fluid—construction."[2] With so little solid footing and much in flux, how can we offer teens something firm? The reign of God points us to a durable sense of narrative, identity, and reality.

A story of suffering. For years, even Christianity has been perceived as an oppressive metanarrative. Postmoderns are understandably critical of such power-hungry, oppressive, grand stories. It makes sense that postmodernism would want to deconstruct such narratives. But the biblical story of God's reign is not that kind of narrative; instead, it calls us to align with God's purposes of shalom, compassion, and justice. The biblical story is one of a God who, out of benevolent intent, called and sent a people to be agents of God's blessing to the world. The story of God's reign in the world is a loving, suffering metanarrative. It's a metanarrative that doesn't grasp and conquer, but seeks to serve, love, and share power; it is sensitive to suffering and pain. The biblical story, therefore, strikes at the heart of deconstruction's fundamental rationale.

Sensitivity to suffering is a major theme of God's sweeping story, shaping the fundamental counter-ideology of God's kingdom. God responds to suffering with compassion (Deuteronomy 26:8) and compassion is central to the law (Exodus 22:22-23; 23:9). The prophets called God's people to embody compassion and justice (Isaiah 58; Amos 5; Micah 6).

Jesus arrived at a time when Israel was being exploited again. The excessive tax system of the Roman Empire and the complex religious structure were oppressing the people.[3] But in that context Jesus taught, "Be merciful, just as your Father is merciful," "love your enemies," and "whoever wants to be great among you must be your servant and whoever wants to be first must be your slave" (Luke 6:36; Matthew 5:43-44; 20:26-27). Like the prophets, Jesus embodied God's concern for the suffering.

The climax of the biblical story is the death and resurrection of Christ (1 Corinthians 15:3-5). The biblical story, captured in God's reign, can be understood as God's extravagant love for a world gone astray. This love led Jesus to the cross—entering into our pain, bearing our suffering and sin.[4]

Empowered self. God's story is an alternative to the postmodern impotence that arises when teens recognize that there is no reliable self that exists at their very core. Since identity is self-constructed, postmoderns will say, one shouldn't hold it tightly or trust it fully. God's story also challenges the leftover sense of modern, conquering autonomy. Modern autonomy places the individual above the community, whereas the biblical story values the individual within community. The modern project of conquest, be it of nature, knowledge, or people, is a quest for power. God's story, however, is one of finding one's true identity in giving up power in order to serve. We are humans created in the image of God for the purpose of advancing God's kingdom purposes through service, compassion, and self sacrifice.

During the exile, Babylon's empire produced both tyrants and victims. The Israelites had two alternatives. One was to see themselves as victims, stripped of dignity and hope. The other alternative was to seek social mobility—to become the privileged. But the exiled Israelites could also recapture a fresh vision of God. They were created in God's image (Genesis 1:26-27). They were not created as afterthoughts, to be slaves to the gods.[5] As agents of God's kingdom, created in God's image, Israel had an alternative self-understanding of themselves as creatures, dependent on their Creator for their existence. This countered the Babylonian values of elitism, social power, and deification.

Jesus modeled this new humanity. He gathered a community of disciples to model an alternative view of power; he commissioned them to go into the entire world as his witnesses, making disciples of all nations (Matthew 28:18-20). The new reality that Jesus inaugurated is the new humanity, renewed in the image of God (Colossians 3:10-11). The work of God's people, as a "chosen nation" and "a people belonging to God," is to help bring about God's rule on the earth (1 Peter 2:9; Revelation 5:9-10).

Our biblical identity as people formed in God's image and called by God offers an alternative, both to the postmodern view of the constructed, decentered self, and to the triumphal modern understanding of humanity. Biblical self identity shatters the false and oppressive alternatives of impotence and power.

Sense of home. A culture of homelessness is also part of our postmodern world. We can't really be "at home" if our reality is only a human construct. In contrast, our relationship with God and the ultimate goodness of creation compels us to call this world our home.

As believers, we are in a covenant relationship with the Creator, responsible for the created order (Genesis 9:9-11). Our role, therefore, is not to dominate or exploit our world; it is to care for it, especially as we hear the voice of the marginalized. In the face of postmodern homelessness, the Scriptures call us to be at home in our world. In ancient Israel, their gift of the land constantly reminded God's people of their covenant relationship. God made it clear that their possession of the land was related to their obedience through doing justice in the land (Deuteronomy 16:20). Over time, however, Israel forgot the land's covenantal character. As a result, the prophets predicted that the unjust would be driven out of the land (1 Kings 21; Isaiah 5:8; Micah 2:1-2; Amos 4).

Jesus came at a time of virtual homelessness as Israel felt the squeeze of Roman oppression. In announcing the arrival of God's kingdom, Jesus established a home that would not be regained by force. This new realm would be characterized by people committed to self-sacrifice and service (Mark 8:35; 9:35; 10:42-44). The way back home was by way of the cross.

This world cannot be our home if we attempt to conquer and control it. It is a gift to be received. We can be at home here as we direct and order creation through self-sacrificial love. In Christ, God made his home among us (John 1:14) and we can find a home in God and God's reign.

To sum up: God's reign is a metanarrative that hears the voice of the marginalized and the suffering. It points to empowered selves among God's people, created in the image of God, to be agents of God's reign. And this story announces that the way of justice and suffering love is the way back home.

A real salvation story in a consumerist world. The reign of God, as a theological paradigm, contrasts with the values of the consumerist narrative that reigns supreme in North America. When Jesus first began announcing the arrival of God's kingdom, he called his hearers to believe in the good news and to repent, to change their minds.[6] Embracing God's reign today requires a radical conversion of the values and behaviors that consumerism embraces.

The good life. The idea of the "good life" in our culture is primarily defined in terms of consumption. Ironically, this very idea may be contributing to a sort of cultural meltdown. In the race for more, marriages are ending and families are falling apart. High levels of stress cause a wide-range of illnesses and self-destructive behaviors among adolescents as well as adults. In God's realm, however, the good life is rooted in spirituality and community, and is characterized by celebration and generosity.[7]

Generosity. Personal accumulation often comes at the expense of others. Oppression and injustice rise when material accumulation is an overriding concern. But Jesus taught that our treasure should be stored in heaven, not on earth. Seeking God's kingdom as our highest aim will ease the anxiousness for things (Matthew 6:19-21, 33). Jesus encouraged his followers to sell all and give to the poor (Luke 12:33; 18:22). When the rich young ruler couldn't do this, he walked away from eternal life. By contrast, Zacchaeus vowed to sell all and live generously. To this Jesus responded, "Today, salvation has come to this house" (see Luke 18:22-23; 19:9). Acts of generosity can liberate us from covetousness and anxiety.[8]

Self-sacrifice. Consumer culture champions the idea that self matters most. But the quest to meet the needs of self is one of the greatest bondages in our society.[9] Jesus affirmed the liberating way of selfless love, self-sacrifice, and service (Mark 9:35; 10:31; John 13). Adolescents can finally lay down the enormous burden of always having to get their own way.

Fulfillment. Our consumer culture explicitly communicates that fulfillment comes from material possessions. But Jesus taught that true fulfillment will come to his followers when they give their lives away. Immediately after he revealed his mission and identity, Jesus said that those who wish to lose their lives for his sake and for the gospel will actually find true life (Mark 8:35; Luke 9:24; Matthew 16:25).

Fulfillment doesn't come from a fickle and rapidly changing market and its definition of "cool." It comes by giving our lives away in the embrace of Christ's gospel and God's mission to the world.

Community. Our culture wants consumers to see themselves first as individuals. If we think of ourselves first without the corrective of community, we are more likely to consume. Jesus, however, modeled community. In the context of community his disciples came to know, love, and imitate Jesus. It was within the first community of disciples where the practical reality of God's kingdom was revealed on earth.[10]

Authentic community offers the support and resources that teenagers need to navigate life. It frees them from encountering life's travails alone. It is in Christian community that young people are able to rescript their narrative, to re-chart their map of reality. Together, they are better able to be formed into the image of Christ.

At many levels, therefore, the biblical reality of God's reign provides a compelling counternarrative to the prevailing narrative of consumer culture. To embrace the kingdom means seeing life in a new way. Living the good life of generosity and self-sacrifice in the context of authentic community brings a kind celebrative fulfillment that consumerism can never offer.

Rescripting the Adolescent Narrative

We've seen how the reign of God engages and challenges the shaping forces of abandonment, postmodernism, and consumer culture. Now, using the four dimensions of God's reign as a framework (chapter 4, and the chart on page 74), let's explore how the counternarrative of God's reign can rewrite the narrative of contemporary adolescents.

The story dimension: embracing a bigger narrative. Family reunions can be awkward occasions. The food is usually good. But the thought of having your cheeks squeezed by your bubbly Aunt Bertha, or listening to reruns of Uncle Ned's grade school misadventures is almost more than you can stand. Then there's the prospect of having to retell your life's story who knows how many times.

But family reunions are important. They give us a sense of something bigger. Not only are we part of a larger family, but we are root-

STORY

IDENTITY

BELONGING

AUTONOMY

Rooted in God's bigger story

Connected to God's people

Authenticated in God's mission

ed in a sense of history. Often, our family stories provide us with a sense of identity—even purpose.

Sarah, an education major in college, was about to graduate in less than a month. She knew she wanted to teach, but something didn't feel right about dealing with over-stressed suburban kids and their hovering, hyper-engaged parents. At a campus gathering, Dr. Keith Phillips, founder of the urban mission, World Impact, told a story of a woman named Mary.

Having grown up as an Alberta farm girl, Mary arrived wide-eyed in south central Los Angeles not long after the Watts riots of 1965. Before long Mary moved into an abandoned building in an urban neighborhood and started a ministry with young mothers. Mary's twenty-plus years of ministry there included children's programs, medical assistance, and teaching. Today Mary's legacy continues. Residents still tell stories of the ways Mary made a difference in that community.

The moment the presentation was over, I watched as Sarah rushed to the front. With tears of joy flowing down her cheeks, she cornered Dr. Phillips and exclaimed, "Mary is my aunt!" Immediately, she signed on to serve with World Impact. Sarah discovered her story. Her new sense of history and identity shaped her life's purpose.

The gospel of the kingdom is one in which Christians tell the story of Jesus' life, death, and resurrection. It is a story of God's mission to bless the world through God's people and to reconcile the world to God. Telling the story of God's reign moves young people from languishing in a sense of storylessness to embracing the story of God and God's people. It weaves their narratives together with the people of God in the Scriptures, Jesus' ministry, the apostles' teaching, and God's future vision for God's people.

Through a kingdom-driven youth ministry, adolescents find themselves entering into the God's larger and still-unfolding story, doing God's work, and inviting others to participate in the drama; they find a clearer sense of identity, a tangible community in which to belong, and a deeper sense of value.

Identity: rooted in God's bigger story. Imagine what happens in the hearts of students when they realize they're part of God's big story. Instead of accepting a fragmented identity, teens find a foundation from which to build their identity. They belong to God, and God has sent them into the world. They also identify with the people of God as agents of God's blessing. Their identity is formed by a relationship with the One who calls them, and it's further shaped by their affinity with God's kingdom people. Together—as a people—they align with God's kingdom purposes.

Also, in a world that seems to peddle a shallow identity of image, teens have the opportunity to embrace God's story of love and compassion. By giving their lives away they can discover who they really are (Matthew 16:25). They are God's, blessed and called, sent to impact the world.

Belonging: connected with God's people. Embracing the story of God's reign means that adolescents belong not only to God, but also to God's people. Together with the church, they are God's beloved children who recognize the depths of God's love for them in Jesus' death and resurrection. The faith community provides a loving and dynamic context for nurture and faith formation.

I remember when Lesli, a high school student, lost her older brother to a tragic farming accident while harvesting wheat in Colorado. As she wrestled with the fairness of life and the goodness of God, the church family wrapped its loving arms around her. In the best way they knew how, caring adults grieved with Lesli and helped her journey through that dark time. Lesli's heartache was expressed in the nurturing environment of the faith community, and her bond with the congregation strengthened as she grew in faith. Teens and adults are called to grow together in unity and faith as they travel life's road. And this oneness, demonstrated in everyday life, genuinely connects teens with God's people.

Autonomy: authenticated in God's missional call. How does God's unfolding story affect adolescents' sense of value and the knowledge that they really matter? First, their sense of value is authenticated by God's call on their lives. They are valued so passionately that Jesus came to earth and lived, died, and rose for them. But a sense of value rises among young people when they realize that God has commissioned them to be agents of healing in the world. Their autonomy continues to grow when they recognize a sense of meaning and purpose in life. They are called to model the reign of God and invite others to participate in that present and coming reality.

The story of God's reign can rescript today's adolescent narrative by solidifying their identity, providing a growing perception of belonging, and a deeper sense of value. Imagine how our teens' hearts will come alive, with awakened souls, as they discover and participate in the unfolding story of God.

The connecting dimension: expanding the circle. The paradigm of God's reign reminds us that while our faith is personal, it's also about community. Teens need to grasp the corporate setting for our faith and understand that they are individuals within community where the gospel is most fully experienced.

Kingdom theology moves teens beyond the limits of individualized faith. When we over-emphasize the personal aspect of faith among

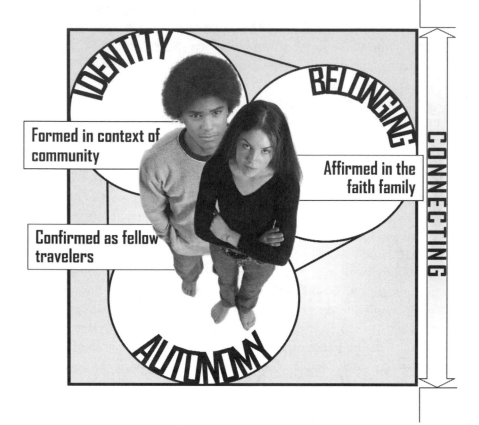

Formed in context of community

Affirmed in the faith family

Confirmed as fellow travelers

IDENTITY   BELONGING   CONNECTING   AUTONOMY

youth, we promote a privatized faith and they become spiritually ego-centric. But when adolescents place their personal spiritual experience within the context of the faith community, a new narrative emerges.

Identity: formed in community context. It is true that an adolescent's identity should come from within, and that it is personal. But it's also true that his or her identity is significantly formed through relationships and in the context of relationships. In fact, I doubt Christianity can be fully expressed individually. The New Testament shows spiritual gifts and the fruit of the Spirit as realities that can only be practiced and appreciated in community. Furthermore, the church's most powerful witness is as a people.

The biblical story is about forming and sending a people as a witness to God's mercy, justice, and love. The first church, seen in Acts 2, demonstrated tangible, loving community. Their winsome peculiarity influenced many to identify with God's new people (v. 47). This reminds the church to claim its formative influence on teens. The body of Christ must be a welcoming, mentoring community.

The faith stories of others, both adults and teens, tremendously influence adolescent identity formation. On a number of occasions I've heard youth leaders share their stories with the youth. Their accounts might be about battling cancer, wrestling with acceptance, or doubting the existence of God. But it never ceases to amaze me that those down-to-earth stories almost always make a lasting impact, more than any of my finely-tuned devotionals. It's not just because the teens identified with the storytellers' struggles. It's because the faith stories wove their way into the growing tapestry of their own narratives.

Belonging: affirmed in the family of faith. A kingdom-centered understanding of faith means that an adolescent's identity cannot be unhooked from the faith community to which they belong. A more widely rooted and broadly connected identity deepens their sense of belonging. The church may not replace the teens' peer clusters, but it can provide a wider contrasting context for relationships. It may even make the desperate need for clusters less necessary.

Think about the practice of baptism. It's more than an outward expression of an inward conviction. It is also a rite of passage that initiates an individual into Christ's body—into God's reign. Through baptism we're saying, "Faith community, I belong to you." It's a covenantal act.

In the summer of 2006, seven bicycle riders and a support crew of three trekked across the United States in an effort to bring faith communities together in conversation. These graduates and students of Eastern Mennonite University thus launched BikeMovement. In part, BikeMovement was about listening to young adults. The movement could give them space to share and a platform to talk to the broader church community about a variety of faith issues. Central to these conversations were questions about what it means to be relevant in our world, and what it means to develop a sense of faith community, both nationally and globally.[11]

BikeMovement illustrates the desire of an emerging generation to embrace a sense of belonging and to know what it means to be a part of a relevant faith community. Congregations have a wonderful opportunity to be intentional about developing this sense of community and belonging. It may be up to our youth ministries to lead the way.

Autonomy: confirmed as fellow-travelers. As the church takes seriously the corporate aspect of God's reign, it can become a community that surrounds its young people with affirmation of their calling. Adults can express the worth of teenagers as fellow travelers on the journey of faith, as future leaders, and as gifted contributors to the current life of the congregation. Adolescents may come to realize that safety and loyalty aren't just found in the underground world. A safe adult world may actually exist.

I'm reminded of Jason and the formative influence of his home church, a rural congregation of thirty. He didn't have the opportunity to attend a dynamic youth program, nor did he participate in any short-term mission trips. But he was an integral part of his church, which he describes as "family." In fact, Jason wouldn't trade his church experience for one with a highly visible youth program. In terms of faith formation, he had all he needed: a caring, mentoring community. Today, Jason and his wife Nancy are church planters in urban St. Louis. I believe his tiny congregation had a lot to do with his sense of meaning and purpose. He loves the church and wants to recreate the sense of true community he remembers from his youth.

This is where smaller churches have a clear advantage. They can't siphon their teens into a youth program disconnected from the world of adults. Out of necessity, the young people are central to the life of the church: taking offering, leading worship, even preaching. Small churches, therefore, need not envy megachurch youth ministries; in some ways such programs contribute to the chasm between the adult world and the adolescent world beneath. Today's adolescents see the highly developed, intricate youth programs as having all the markings of adult systems. Teens dismiss them—in some cases unfairly—as products of adult-driven agendas.

The narrative of God's reign recaptures the communal nature of the faith experience. It enables young people to embrace the richness of the faith community, which forms a living lab for their faith journey. Since today's teens are predisposed to community, this opportunity must not be lost.

Transforming dimension: engaging in authentic change. When we say yes to Jesus, we are changed. We are new creations. The old is gone and the new has arrived (2 Corinthians 5:17). But as personal change takes root, it should lead to a desire to make a bigger difference in the world. Deepening levels of personal change include commitment to societal transformation. The kingdom counternarrative is able to move teens beyond individual transformation to social impact.

Let us clarify one assumption, however, which has to do with *how* broader change occurs within the framework of God's reign. Following the model and teaching of Christ, Christians are not called

to use the world's coercive power strategies to extend God's reign. God, who reigns in love, intends to bless the whole earth. This God has extended an invitation to all humanity to receive the gift of God's reign in their lives. Ultimately, Jesus' work on the cross discloses God's compassionate strategy for engaging the world. The cross of Christ is God's claim to this world. This claim is not that of a tyrant grasping for greater power. It's that of a lover deeply desiring to love and be loved, liberating God's beloved from false masters.[12] The way to societal change is through sacrificial love and service.

Identity: solidified as a change agent. When teens enter the kingdom, they have the opportunity to experience the formative power of change. We know that personal change shapes their identity, but what about broader, bigger change? In the Sermon on the Mount, Jesus used the metaphors of salt and light to illustrate the identity of his followers. Both images are quiet but powerful change agents. Salt, a stable compound, changes whatever it touches. In the battle of light and darkness, light always wins. You can never out-dark light. But Jesus connects these two metaphors to one's identity: "You *are* the salt of the earth. . . . You *are* the light of the world" (Matthew 5:13, 14, emphasis added). Jesus didn't say "You are like salt or light." Or, "You should try to be light or salt." Being a change agent is part of our DNA as believers. And the scope of change is global. We are the salt of *the earth*, the light of *the world*. We are called to make a difference everywhere.

This is a departure from the typical adolescent narrative. Identity does not come from being like everyone else, displaying the latest, coolest, and trendiest. For Christian youth, identity is somehow discovered as they swim upstream against the flow of prevailing culture. Also, teens' identity is not formed from the outside-in through personal accumulation. They experience Christ-like kingdom identity as they give their lives away.

Belonging: clarified as a contrast culture. Teenagers who embrace the kingdom counternarrative experience a new sense of belonging. They now belong to a competing culture—a people that lives out an upside-down ethic as far as the world is concerned.

As this sense of belonging takes hold, teens begin to understand what it means to be a royal priesthood, a holy nation, a people belonging to God (1 Peter 2:9). Adolescents start to embrace the idea that they are part of a people called and sent to bless the world (Genesis 12:1-3). This is where allegiance language becomes so important. Young people don't belong to those brands that champion external adornment. They belong to a people of authentic, deep change. Their primary allegiance doesn't have to be with clusters of teens desperately searching for safety. Their ultimate allegiance is to God. They're part of a people with purpose, helping to establish safety, justice, and Shalom in the world.

Autonomy: developed as participants in God's call. A deep sense of worth comes to us as we make a difference in the world. The short-term youth missions movement is based on that idea. Not long ago Jessica and Heidi, two young teens from a small Mennonite Brethren church, returned from a short-term mission assignment in Malawi, Africa. For three weeks, the sole task of their team was to wash the feet of village children and give them proper fitting shoes. For their selfless work they received plenty of cheerful smiles and big hugs, and they sweated a lot. But this isn't the first mission trip these girls have taken—and it probably won't be their last. Heidi and Jessica are blossoming as they follow Christ. They have a growing belief that they matter because of God's call on their lives to serve and to love. When teens participate in the transforming power of God's reign, their sense of autonomy develops.

Future-now dimension: embodying God's world. The kingdom of God is eschatological—a current reality that points to a future culmination. A kingdom theology can enable students to live out their faith in the context of community in such a way that others are given a snapshot of God's intended future.

As the primary agent of God's reign, the church is something like a pioneering community. Its purpose is to live in fellowship with God, each other, and creation, pointing in the direction that God is taking history.[13] Among the pioneers are teens who understand they are modeling God's desired future. Adolescents can align their lives with God's goal and travel along God's trajectory. They, alongside God's people, become a visible sign of God's world.

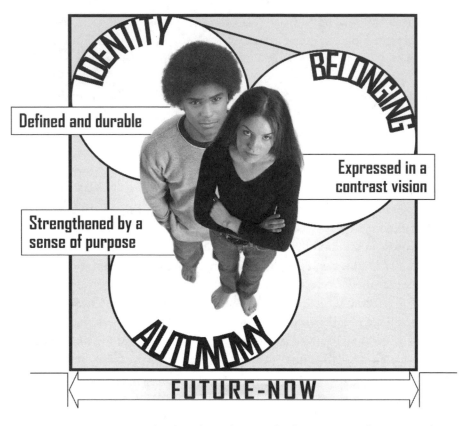

In Jesus' prayer for his disciples we find a strategy for our eschatological engagement with the world. Jesus prays that while his disciples are not of the world, he has sent them into the world (John 17:13-18). Christians are to be *in* the world, but not *of* the world; as God's people we are an alternative, eschatological culture. As we seek to influence the world by being God's people and by *not* conforming to the world's patterns, we are eschatological. We live the truth of the gospel as we model reconciliation, compassion, and self-giving love. We change our world as our example makes an impact on it.

Identity: defined and durable. This future-now aspect of the kingdom requires a deep level of faith and maturity. To be a tangible sign of God's future reign emphasizes actions, behaviors, and allegiances. Consider the amount of resolve it takes to model the kingdom in the midst of real life. Being the kingdom now not only points to the future of God, but it speaks into the present, where prevailing values are different. Like the ancient prophets, adolescents who critique the present by living out a distinct future will encounter opposition.

Teens who represent God's vision for the future personify change. And we all know how much people like change. It takes courage to actually take sides in a family dispute, a classroom discussion, or a political debate. You openly side with someone, or with one viewpoint over against another. When teenagers—or any of us for that matter—intentionally model God's future reign, they're taking sides, defining who they are—and that may not always be popular.

A number of years ago, our youth group participated in a mission trip in Chicago with the Center for Student Missions. It was an eye-opening, life-changing week for many of my students. On the final day, as a way to seal the experience, we went to the planetarium. On Lake Shore Drive, beneath Chicago's skyline, we gathered to pray. Hand in hand and with heads bowed, we prayed that God would bless our efforts and move in the city. Within moments I heard some catcalls in the distance. I discretely opened one eye, cocked my head, and discovered that it came from a group of heckling teens. But they didn't stop at that. They hid behind a wall and hurled trash and crushed beer cans, hitting several of my students on the back. We weren't handing out tracts, or standing on soap boxes preaching doom and gloom, but we were making a statement, and we were noticed. Our quiet actions identified us as Christians, and at least on that day, our presence was not appreciated.

At this level, teens' understanding of who they are is not found in the status quo, or with the hottest brands. When adolescents signal a world in which God rules, it is most likely the result of a deep, durable faith. Their actions flow out of a clearly defined sense of identity.

Belonging: expressed in a contrast vision. Modeling God's reign in the midst of the world stems from a clear sense of belonging. Those who desire to live out God's alternative reality must have a solid grasp of the contrast kingdom vision, and that includes knowing that they belong to God, and to the people of God.

Three years ago, at the age of twelve, Zach Hunter became passionate about freeing slaves. Knowing that the slave trade is alive and well today, Zach started raising money to end slavery with a campaign called "Loose Change to Loosen Chains." Now, in his new book, *Be the Change*, he's calling on his generation, and all believers, to abolish slavery in the name of Christ.[14] It seems clear that Zach's slave-freeing zeal and his passion to summon a new generation of abolitionists comes from a clear sense of belonging to a people and a vision that is much bigger than a peer cluster.

While their peer clusters are still valuable, adolescents, like Zach, can know that they have a deep identity with God's kingdom people. When young people invest in kingdom-driven living, soon the luster of brands fades. The grip of the cluster weakens. Their sense of belonging has been captured by a greater vision.

Autonomy: strengthened by a sense of purpose. When teens embrace the vision of what God plans to do in the world, their sense of autonomy deepens. Meaning and value surge from an emerging sense of purpose. I think of Isaac, who came to Tabor College to complete a ministry degree. His call to ministry was deeply affected by his teen mission and service experiences and the influence of his home congregation. As I heard his story, I could tell that his depth of character, ministry focus, and kingdom resolve came from a strong sense of purpose. I knew that his self-worth did not come from his image or style. It didn't come from a tenuous bond with disoriented peers, or from the approval of self-interested adults. Isaac found value in kingdom purposes.

Young people who follow God's vision understand that, as God's kingdom people, they are "first fruits" of that kingdom; they model the beginning of what is to come. The future-now dimension of God's reign communicates to the world what God plans to do, because it shows that God is already doing it. There's no greater purpose than God's reign to infuse a healthy sense of value and autonomy.

Ideas for Scripting the Kingdom Counternarrative

If the reign of God offers adolescents a contrast narrative, how does the faith community as a whole embody and express the kingdom counternarrative among its teens? What follows are some prac-

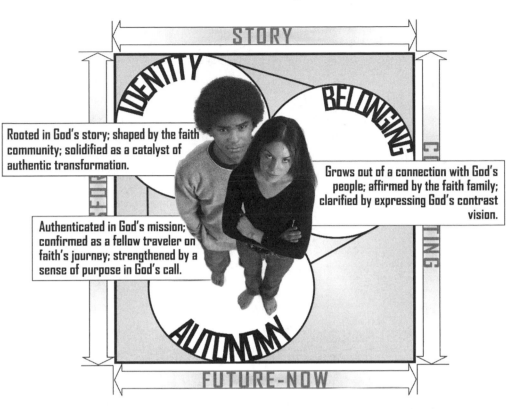

STORY

IDENTITY

BELONGING

Rooted in God's story; shaped by the faith community; solidified as a catalyst of authentic transformation.

Grows out of a connection with God's people; affirmed by the faith family; clarified by expressing God's contrast vision.

Authenticated in God's mission; confirmed as a fellow traveler on faith's journey; strengthened by a sense of purpose in God's call.

AUTONOMY

FUTURE-NOW

tical ideas for a youth ministry that flows from kingdom theology.

Come alongside teens. In a world in which teens feel forced to navigate adolescent life on their own, the church is a place where abandonment and isolation should not exist. *First*, the adults in the church can move toward forming relationships with teens. It could include seeking out young people before or after a worship gathering; being present at important school events; finding multiple ways to affirm them through cards, emails, or text messages; or recruiting a greater number of adult volunteers in the youth ministry. Simply with their words and their time, adults can provide a congruent message of love, caring, and hope. This in itself is radically counter to our prevailing culture.

Second, the church can begin to provide developmental markers that communicate that their teens are growing toward healthy adulthood. For example, when adolescents receive their driver's license, the church can recapture it as a rite of passage, conferring on them the responsibilities that come with new freedoms. As a part of the church's liturgy, markers could be as simple as a blessing when teens reach a particular age. They could also come in the form of weekend retreats in which young women or men are affirmed and invited to participate more fully in adult roles, responsibilities, and decisions. These markers can re-infuse certain achievements with meaning.

Third, the church can connect teens with spiritually growing mentors. Besides the relationships that ensue, mentoring also helps to incorporate these maturing adolescents into the life of the faith community.

Offer a climate of safety and belonging. The church can create a culture that is *for* their teens. When the church rediscovers the values of community, adolescents are able to find an environment in which they belong and feel safe. We must allow teens to be real; to ask risky, hard questions about life and faith without our passing judgment on them. We can tell stories of our own struggles. Adolescents will realize that we're not as different from them as they assumed. Teens are trying to understand themselves and this Jesus they're supposed to follow—and it's hard. Knowing that we are on their side, creating a safe place for them, will reduce their sense of abandonment.

To foster such a climate, we can create more venues that bring adults and teens together, opening spaces for the purpose of hearing and telling stories. For instance, instead of just heading home after a service project, reserve a room at a local restaurant and design the table conversation to include storytelling: your most embarrassing moments, your favorite vacation, what got, or gets, you in trouble as a teen.

Authentic community supports and resources teenagers as they navigate life. They no longer have to encounter life's travails alone. In a safe, Christian community young people are able to re-chart their map of reality where they are more intentionally formed into the image of Christ.

Support and empower parents. Youth ministries have an important role in supporting the students' family systems. When adolescents begin to perceive the family as just another—and sometimes hostile—

adult system, youth workers can equip parents in making the home a safer, more nurturing environment. For example, youth leaders can encourage parents to practice the art of listening, not just hearing, but truly attending to their youth with understanding. It's vital that parents remember their own trials of growing up as a teen. But they also need to recognize the unique hurdles adolescents face today. Parents could ask their child, "What's it like to be (fill in the age)? I've forgotten." As parents listen they will develop a deeper level of compassion for their child's adolescent journey.

Parents also need to be empowered to set appropriate boundaries for their teenagers. Boundaries are negotiated fences that guide their children toward adulthood. These rules, consequences, or other forms of discipline are designed to protect their teens, but also to curb unwise decisions and young, self-centered attitudes. Setting boundaries centers around the notion of guidance and negotiation rather than punishment and unilateral decrees. Setting boundaries can be helpful with most teenage behavior or attitude that needs adjustment.

One way to empower parents in this way is to bring them together for a retreat or an afternoon seminar. Do some role-playing that models parent-teen conversations. Here's a scenario. "Spencer, why is it that you can't seem to find the time to finish your homework or do chores around the house?" "I don't know." "Your dad and I think it's because you spend too much time with your XBOX and on Facebook with your friends. Is that true?" "I guess." "So, you can either stay off Facebook for a week or let us have your XBOX for a week, until you show us that you're getting your work done. What'll it be?" "Umm . . . XBOX, I guess." "Then next week, we'll see how things stand." By exploring such scenarios, parents can share their own experience and exchange ideas. Mutual support goes a long way.

Parents can help their adolescents move toward adulthood by helping their teens put their faith into practice. By helping to facilitate service opportunities, for example, parents model for their teens how to think beyond themselves. When they work alongside their children, parents have a point of contact for genuine dialogue. What would happen when a teen asks, "Why is the rescue mission's dining hall mostly full of ethnic minorities?" Imagine the rich conversations around social justice issues that might arise. As teens become sensitive to the needs of others, they'll practice the ethic of Jesus and learn to function as interdependent individuals.

Solidify meaning and identity. In a world that seems devoid of real meaning and true identity, we can significantly shape adolescents' sense of who they are. For example, Ministry Quest, a program of Mennonite Brethren Biblical Seminary, is designed to help youth ministries do just that. (The program is similar to the !Explore program of Associated Mennonite Biblical Seminary and the LEAP program of Eastern Mennonite Seminary.) Geared for Canadian and American high school students ages sixteen to eighteen who are curious about God's call and ministry, Ministry Quest helps teens explore possibilities in ministry and leadership by integrating their love for God, their gifts, and their passions. Along with a number of retreats, a centerpiece of the program, is a relationship with a mentor from the students' local church. Together, the student and mentor wrestle with the realities of living out God's call in the midst of life.

Dozens of Mennonite Brethren congregations are capturing the vision of Ministry Quest, transforming lives through the power of God's call. These churches are affirming their teens, connecting them with a range of caring adults, and intentionally solidifying their sense of meaning and identity. Chloe, a recent Ministry Quest graduate, always knew she wanted to serve God, but wasn't sure how. During a retreat, God's quiet call to elementary education became clear after she heard the call stories of adult mentors and other teens.

Youth ministries can also invite teens to participate in God's new reality by organizing a student retreat specifically to help teens identify and articulate their own call story. As the story emerges they soon realize that they're an important part of God's people who have been chosen and sent by God to be agents of God's reign. Simply by understanding that they are a people who belong to God, offering an alternative reality to the world, they can develop a coherent sense of self.

Practice service. Our consumer culture says that our identity comes by way of acquisition and possession. But in God's kingdom, our identity comes from identifying with the crucified Christ and acknowledging God's identification with us.[15] As participants in God's reign, we are part of a people called and sent by God to be agents of God's blessing, mercy, and compassion to the world.

One effective way to solidify adolescent identity is to participate in the sacrificial practice of selfless love, service, and compassion. We can retool service projects and mission trips by framing the youth's activities in terms of a discovery of who they are in God. By asking the question "What did you learn about who you are and who Jesus called you to be?" we invite teens to follow the ministry of Christ and to model the kingdom ethics of justice and compassion. Through this combination of service and reflection, the teens' identity is renewed and Christ's identity becomes their own.[16]

Experience the truth. In today's postmodern world, experienced truth is "embodied" truth. Teens have a strong desire to experience truth personally, not simply by reading or hearing about things. And this longing is biblical. More than a set of beliefs to be grasped, truth is a person (John 14:6). It can be experienced in relationship with Christ. The practice of daily discipleship, therefore, lends itself to the postmodern search for experienced truth. By following the way of Jesus, truth can be embodied and lived.

Instead of just talking about being a peacemaker, for example, youth leaders can analyze a case study or do a role-play that pits individuals or groups against each other. After reflecting on students' reactions and emotions, they can use the exercise as a teachable moment by asking, "How would a redemptive peacemaking response change the situation?" Even better, youth leaders can arrange for teens to accompany mediators in community disputes, such as a conflict between a teen gang member and a store owner whose property was tagged with graffiti. Let teens experience truth and see it in action first-hand.

Be authentic. The adolescent search for authenticity must translate into ministry practice. A reign-of-God paradigm can help youth ministries shift from being simply "relevant" to being real. Teens know that life is complex and sometimes heart-breaking. They are wary of, and brand as false, a gospel that sells Jesus as a step toward personal success and fulfillment. Our devotionals or Bible studies with youth, therefore, need not avoid life's tough issues. What does it mean to forgive an abusive parent? How can we find a way to live for Christ and still have serious questions about God's power in the world? How do we cope with the anguish and guilt of an addiction? These are real life issues. If we don't deal with them, who will? And we can address them in the context of faith and loving community.

Rescripting with a kingdom narrative means we hear the painful cries of today's teens, taking the time to truly understand the complexities of their lives. We give them resources, such as adult friendships, to get through life. By giving voice to their suffering and acknowledging that God, life and the world are mysterious, we model a credible alternative to the isolation and abandonment that they experience.

Authentic youth leaders see themselves as co-travelers on the journey of faith. As a part of an authentic community, the people of God, we emphasize "ministry *with*," not "ministry *to*." Authenticity appears in our own "life lived," rather than a mere "precept believed." Youth ministry thus moves beyond mere belief, and includes transformation and conversion.

Recapture community. Postmodern adolescents are driven to community for answers, and their sense of abandonment has only deepened that desire. Fortunately, it is in the context of the wider community that truth and life are experienced. Rescripting the adolescent story with a kingdom narrative ultimately means we embrace teens as an integral part of the faith community—an expression of the people of God. Together, we all navigate the storms of life. Together, we help create meaning, identity, and a sense of purpose as we invite others to participate in the radical reality of God's reign.

Our culture's consuming narrative depends on the assumption that individualistic needs are primary, feeding the notion of the therapeutic self. This notion, focused on individual solutions to life's challenges, runs counter to both the adolescent desire for community and the communal nature of the church as an agent of God's reign. Youth ministries can model the communal character of God's reign by forming interpretive communities that help teens reflect on the world around them. This can be accomplished as a multitude of adults surrounds teens in a variety of ways. Small groups can be retooled to practice accountability and being Jesus to friends, rather than focusing mainly on intellectual content. Intergenerational activities and mentoring relationships can help adults and teens hear each others stories, fears, and dreams.

The church must renew its focus on the kingdom value of community. By embodying the kingdom in the context of community, youth ministries can create a new framework of meaning that stands in clear contrast to consumerism's vision of reality.

Create sacred space. The busyness and clutter produced by popular culture's media onslaught demands too much of teens' time and offers countless distractions. The rush and rhythm of consumer culture makes it very difficult for adolescents to tune in to God, develop their true identity, and be formed in their faith. Participating in God's reign, however, means taking the time to learn how to follow Jesus in life in order to love and know God personally.

In the context of community, youth ministries can influence teens to recreate and rediscover "sacred space." This means not only exposing the destructive nature of the consumer narrative; it involves the practice of "dehabituation."[17] Jesus modeled dehabituation as he moved back and forth between time with people and time alone, between moments of self-giving and moments of recapturing spiritual energy from God (Mark 4:35-39; Luke 11:1-13). The ascetic practices of fasting, silence, solitude, and frugality enable teens to reduce the distractions of their world in order to reflect on who they are as children of God. This might mean taking students to a remote mountain retreat or a quiet lake, with no agenda. There, for a short time, they can replace the hectic rhythms of everyday life with moments of keen awareness of God. Youth ministries should also find ways to integrate these practices into their programs. Without conscious efforts to create such space, youth may drift aimlessly with the currents of daily life instead of deliberately choosing to live as part of God's reign.

Find true fulfillment. The narrative of consumer culture tells adolescents that fulfillment comes through material possession. But the same narrative conveys that one can never have enough. Ironically, the source of fulfillment never satisfies. Moreover, consumption and acquisition often come at the expense of others.

In God's reign, however, fulfillment does not come from possession and acquisition; it comes through self-sacrifice and generosity. By losing one's life, by giving it away, one finds new life (Matthew 16:24-26). Youth ministries can rescript the consumption narrative and model the kingdom by following Jesus in acts of service and generosity. Short-term mission trips and service projects, when coupled with instructive debriefing sessions, can be powerful tools that help teens discover their source of true fulfillment.

Practice discernment. In his book *Practicing Discernment with Youth*, David White argues for discernment as an approach to youth ministry. Discernment brings the gospel in conversation with our lives and our culture in a way that awakens the whole person.[18]

First, White suggests that we create a listening space for teens to express their heart themes—their joys, struggles, longings, and dreams. Second, we should help adolescents wrestle with seeing the world accurately as both complex and full of potential. Third, by remembering (in prayer) and dreaming (seeing a future cultivated by the Christian story), teens are better able to live from their soul, above their superficial, distorted culture. Finally, White advocates action. Teens must be given the opportunity to do something to express their desire to make a tangible and positive difference in the world. If their passion is mission, send them to Asia or Africa to intern with a missionary team that your church supports. If some youth are sensitive to the wiles of consumerism, empower them to refocus your congregation during Advent with worship that is marked by compassion rather than consumption.[19]

Like growing a healthy tree or a fruitful garden, discernment in teens requires cultivation, with constant attention and nurture. When young people practice discernment by bringing the story of God's reign into conversation with their world, they can better find their way through the ordeals of adolescence and toward a biblical understanding of who they're called to be.

Practice meaningful dialogue. Hand in hand with discernment, perhaps the most effective way youth workers can become players in the culture-wide contest of teen influence is through intentional and meaningful dialogue. The consumer narrative can tell a very convincing story, but it must be engaged and countered by the equally convincing story of the gospel. Through careful conversation and interpretive dialogues, caring Christian adults can expose the insidious nature of the consuming narrative, replacing it with the redemptive story of God's reign.

For example, youth leaders might generate conversations about the importance of character, contrasting consumer character with Christian character. The consumer character is defined by insatiability. Our consumer culture teaches teens never to be satisfied—at least for long. By contrast, Christian character is very wary of greed. The only insatiable desire that a Christian ought to have is for God (Psalm 42:1), not created things. Consumerism disorders that desire, and it can easily become idolatry.

One useful exercise to generate dialogue about consumerism is to take teens on a field trip through a shopping mall. Leaders would have them identify the ways in which retailers entice them to buy, then in a careful debriefing session, having them compare their mall experience with Paul's notion of contentment (Philippians 4:11-13). The session can include the telling of real-life stories of how liberating it is to be satisfied with what you have. The conversation should consider the issue of character—both consumer and Christian—as well as the ways in which consumerism has grasped control of our society's stories and shaped our values.

Conclusion

The reign of God has enough depth and force to rescript today's adolescent narrative. Postmodern deconstruction has today's adolescents wrestling with an acute sense of lostness and the fragmentation of self. The salvation narrative of consumption has deceived contemporary teens into believing that their identity and source of fulfillment come with a price tag. Systemic abandonment has forced our young people to seek shelter underground, apart from the hostilities of the adult world. They are lost, hurt, and searching for answers, with few adults available to provide honest answers.

This is a time of great opportunity and challenge for those in youth ministry. The wounds of teens are deep and in need of healing. With God's reign as a guiding paradigm, local youth ministries can rewrite the adolescent story by creating a competing, contrast culture in the context of community. Within the framework of authentic relationships, an alternative story of God's kingdom can be told.

A Grid for Assessing Kingdom-Driven Youth Ministry

Erica couldn't believe what just happened. As she watched Jasmine, Miguel, Jordan, and Erin leave the coffee shop, she could hardly contain her exhilaration. She expected her early morning youth leadership team meeting to be one more in a long string of the usual: a short devotional, a time of prayer, and some planning for the next month—but not today.

For years Erica, a dedicated youth volunteer, had prayed and hoped that this day would come. Erica's leadership team had just blind-sided her with a dream, a kingdom vision. They wanted to start a ministry to elderly people in their town. The teens had noticed that too many were unable to get out of the house to run errands or keep up with their yards. Some weren't eating well. The team wanted to organize an effort among the teens in their community that would help the senior population with basics of everyday life: buying groceries, mowing lawns, paying bills, or picking up prescriptions. It was an ambitious vision, but they were energized.

When Erica asked, "Where did this idea come from?" Jordan, a high school senior, replied, "What do you mean? You've been teaching us all this stuff about the kingdom and being a blessing for so long. I guess it just finally clicked."

"Could it actually be that these entertainment-driven, pop-icon-wannabe teens have a new outlook on life and faith?" she thought. Erica recalled past youth sessions about God's big story, and the difficulty of helping her students to find their place in it. She remembered how fleeting the sense of community had been. One week the youth meeting would be saturated with a feeling of connectedness. The next week, self-focused individualism would rear its ugly head—again.

Maybe the turnaround came after their mission trip with S.W.A.P. (Sharing With Appalachian People), to the coal-mining town of Harlan, tucked away in the mountains of Kentucky. On that trip the students began to realize that their own lives were changed as they shared their lives with the local folks. A new desire had seized the youth: a desire to express the compassion, sacrifice, and love of Christ wherever they found themselves—even at home. However it happened, today Erica recognized that her teens were "getting it."

Imagine the influence of a youth ministry guided by the biblical paradigm of God's reign. Teens' lives are eternally changed. Students transform their culture because they know what it means to participate in God's mission to the world.

In the previous chapters we've briefly described today's adolescent narrative and offered the reign of God as a biblical alternative to that narrative. But how does the reign-of-God paradigm translate to youth ministry strategies? In this concluding chapter we'll identify some important markers of a kingdom-driven youth ministry, especially in light of the developmental needs of adolescents. We will discuss the value of a mission statement. Finally, from these foundations, we will construct an evaluative grid for developing and evaluating a youth ministry that is clearly shaped by God's reign.

Markers of a Kingdom-Driven Youth Ministry

To effectively touch teens' lives, a youth ministry must carefully consider youth culture. But it must also adopt a *theological* framework that guides the ministry in proclaiming the gospel in that cultural context. The kingdom of God can provide that grid. What does a kingdom-driven youth ministry value? What are the markers of a kingdom-driven youth ministry? Youth ministries focused on a "reign-of-God vision" move toward kingdom-driven methodology, demonstrated by several defining markers. Taken individually, these markers aren't necessarily unique to kingdom-driven youth ministry, as a package they are distinctive.

1. A kingdom-driven youth ministry asserts God's sovereignty. Kingdom-driven youth ministries *understand and communicate that God is sovereign over all things.* Proclaiming God's authority and activity in all things, past, present and future, affirms that God is more than Creator; God participates in human history. It asserts that God continues to be active in the world, in the church, and in our lives. Sensationalized news media coverage and global crises can paint a picture of a chaotic world. But, when discussing current events, youth workers should consistently remind teens that God remains in control. They can continue to pray that God's will be done on earth, just as it is in heaven.

2. It reiterates God's bigger story. A youth ministry guided by God's reign tells the story of a people called and sent by God to bless the world, agents of God's grace and reconciliation. This is a narrative that counters the storylessness of postmodern deconstruction. It offers meaning to life and can move teens toward a more biblical sense of identity. It's not enough to root a youth ministry in exegetical references to isolated Bible stories and Scripture verses, a practice that only fragments the gospel. To bring cohesion and clarity to the Scriptures, activities such as worship music, Bible studies, and discussions should regularly make connections to God's larger narrative and to teens' part in that story. For example, youth leaders can place the Old Testament stories such as the call of Abram (Genesis 12:1-3) or Jacob's wrestling with God (Genesis 32:22-32) in the context of how God has called and sent God's people throughout history— including the youth—to be a blessing. They can explain how the prophets sharply criticized God's people for not being a blessing (for example in Isaiah 58), or how Jesus' ministry and Paul's writings included the formation of a community that would bless the world.

3. It affirms Jesus' kingdom launch. A youth ministry shaped by kingdom paradigm affirms that Jesus inaugurated God's reign. In Christ, God's empire became present and visible in love and compassion. God's reign is "the kingdom of our Lord" (Revelation 11:15). Jesus was "the decisive inbreaking of the kingdom into human history."[1] This means that youth can position themselves as participants in the end-time people of God, helping to represent the visible, alternative, and parallel society that Jesus announced. This marker implies a balance between the gospel *about* Christ (his death on the cross for our sins) with the gospel *of* Christ (his kingdom invitation). A good way to affirm this orientation is to spend time with Jesus' kingdom parables and to emphasize his ethics of love and care for the weak and vulnerable.

4. It acknowledges a two-world tension. A kingdom-driven youth ministry recognizes that the reign of God is at odds with the regime of this world. The "ruler of the power of the air" continues to be at work (Ephesians 2:2). The church's struggle is ultimately against the "spiritual forces of evil in the heavenly places" (Ephesians 6:12). Christians find themselves battling on a number of fronts: from one's inner thought life and daily behaviors to culture, politics, and economics that conflict with kingdom values. Youth workers, therefore, are called to lead youth in an engagement with the world that is marked by a creative tension. This will happen whenever the youth compare kingdom values with the cultural assumptions they face every day; for example, in a discussion of a movie where youth affirm positive aspects that are consistent with kingdom values, yet also critique the more harmful elements. In such encounters there will be both a healthy suspicion of culture and a compassion for the world.[2]

5. It pledges ultimate allegiance to God. A youth ministry sensitive to God's reign demonstrates that the believer's primary allegiance belongs to God and God's kingdom. When we enter God's reign, all other allegiances become secondary. Jesus made this clear when he commanded, "Give . . . to the emperor the things that are the emperor's, and to God the things that are God's" (Matthew 22:21). Our allegiance to God's reign, therefore, supersedes our allegiance to nation, school, or favorite sports franchise. This means youth leaders guard their political rhetoric and their loyalty language. Unqualified nationalism or allegiance to political parties have no place in the kingdom. Nor do displays of fanatic devotion to professional and college sports teams, or blind loyalty to corporate brands.

Living Jesus' non-violent way of peace will be a countercultural act in a culture that glorifies violence, especially when the state campaigns for war. Kingdom-driven youth workers will help youth wrestle with what it means to practice Christian citizenship, but they will also support their youth in conscientious objection to military service by pursuing alternative service, say, to the victims of violence and oppression. Our first allegiance belongs to God, and we must help youth make difficult choices when loyalties conflict.

6. It expresses discipleship as following Jesus. A kingdom-driven youth ministry will affirm that participating in God's reign means following Jesus daily. Jesus is the norm for living. His life, ministry, and teaching provide a model for kingdom ethics in daily life. Christians are called to follow in Christ's steps, walking as Jesus did (1 Peter 2:21; 1 John 2:6). When current events intensify cultural debate, youth workers should continually ask, "What does Jesus teach us on this issue? What would Jesus do?" Biblical instruction should begin with Jesus; his teaching is the primary lens through which the Bible, life, and the world are understood.

7. It demonstrates compassionate kingdom ethics. A youth ministry driven by the paradigm of God's reign understands that kingdom ethics include compassion, self-sacrifice, selfless love, service, and an emphasis on authentic community. These are ethics embodied by Christ in his earthly ministry, ethics he called his followers to embrace here and now. They are the rules of engagement, the "way" of the kingdom (see Matthew 5:38-48; Mark 10:13-16; John 13:1-17). Acting in ways contrary to these, such as using violence, oppression, injustice, selfishness, accumulation, or individualism is to forsake the kingdom. Instead, youth ministries should lead the way in service. Mission trips and other compassion-driven projects should be central to youth ministry programming because they teach and model kingdom ethics.

8. It lives out a new reality. Those involved in a kingdom-conscious youth ministry believe that those who seek God's reign engage the prevailing culture by showing the world a new reality and inviting others to participate in it.

Jesus lived out a radically new realm that was already breaking into the old, calling would-be followers to join in (Mark 8:34-39). Think about the social norms Jesus broke when he asked the woman at the well for a drink (John 4:7). Conversing in public with a promiscuous Samaritan woman in Samaria was way outside the Jewish religious box—especially for someone considered a rabbi. Jesus never gave a second thought to healing on the Sabbath (Mark 3:1-6; Luke 13:10-17), another life-denying rule of the time. Jesus' ultimate invitation to a life of sacrificial love and compassion was given on the cross.

This marker of the new reality encourages us regularly to connect what teens are doing now with God's unfolding future. For instance, while debriefing after a mission trip or while leading in times of prayer, we can remind youth of God's eschatological goals for humanity: that our participation in God's work now is part of the future that God is creating.

9. It embraces the church's role in the kingdom. A youth ministry guided by God's reign affirms that the church, while not the kingdom, is God's primary agent for its emergence. God's reign extends beyond the local congregation, but local faith communities are called to embody God's new reality. As the church spreads and grows, God's reign unfolds in greater fullness. To teach this reality, youth leaders can help youth get involved in the kingdom ministries of their own congregation, or take students on a tour of local ministries that the church performs, such as food banks, homeless shelters, or evangelistic outreach projects. In the activity's debrief, emphasize that these local ministries are participating in God's reign—there's a kingdom connection.

While there are probably other markers of kingdom-driven youth ministries, these are significant. To be kingdom-driven a youth ministry is to help teens—through its relationships, teaching, and programs—understand that God has called and sent them to be a blessing to the world. Jesus, the inaugurator of God's reign, is their model for a life of compassion, self-sacrifice, justice, and generosity. Following Jesus moves young people beyond the experience of personal change to participation in societal transformation. This journey is possible because they are part of a community that demonstrates an alternative reality in the midst of culture, calling others to join in the celebrative, generous, compassionate living.

Mission Statement

In addition to these markers, it is also helpful to consider the value of a mission statement as a foundation for the evaluative grid that we will construct for kingdom-driven youth ministry. A mission statement can be an external public relations piece, but, more importantly, it is useful as a road map for the ministry itself. It also helps evaluate the ministry by determining whether or not the destination has been reached. It is important, therefore, for any youth ministry strategy to include a clear articulation of its mission, understood by those engaged in the ministry. Mission statements that reflect the paradigm of God's reign should express the ever-widening spheres of faith: personal, corporate, and societal.

Each youth ministry will shape a mission statement that fits its own context, so we won't even present models here. However, three evaluative questions are useful in shaping such a statement:

- In what ways is our youth ministry developing journey-conscious followers of Jesus?
- How are we integrating adolescents into the family of faith?
- To what extent is our youth ministry helping teens embody and participate in God's reign as a contrast culture?

The first question emphasizes the *personal* level of discipleship and spiritual growth. Developing passionate, journey-conscious followers of Jesus affirms that a growing relationship with Jesus is at the center of faith—and central to the youth ministry, too. Jesus personifies God's reign and provides a model for kingdom living.

The second question stresses the vital *corporate* component of one's faith. Integrating adolescents into the body of Christ affirms the value of community. Too often, youth ministries move teens away from the body of Christ and contribute to the culture of abandonment that teens already experience. Countercultural though it might be, an effective youth ministry in today's adolescent context must move teens toward adulthood as fully functioning, interdependent participants in the faith community.

The third question draws attention to the *societal* element of one's witness in the world. Helping teens embody and participate in the contrast culture of God's reign means following Jesus in personal transformation and moving toward societal change. In keeping with Jesus' model, this is done by showing the world a new reality of compassion, justice, and self-sacrificial love, and inviting others to enter this radically contrast culture.

A youth ministry that embraces kingdom values should find a way to articulate all three spheres of faith in its mission statement. But even after a statement has been formed, the task of keeping the ministry on track remains. How will youth workers make sure that the ministry is speaking to the developmental needs of the youth, as well as to their postmodern adolescent culture? These questions are at the heart of the following evaluation grid.

A Kingdom-Driven Youth Ministry Grid

The Kingdom-Driven Youth Ministry Grid presented here is intended to help youth workers both evaluate and strengthen viable youth ministry models by integrating the biblical paradigm of God's reign. The grid emphasizes a two-fold tension. First, it takes context seriously by enabling youth ministries to be developmentally appropriate and culturally discerning. Second, it takes seriously the mandate to be biblically faithful by helping youth ministries align with God's larger story. At the same time, the grid is designed to help move adolescents beyond an individualized faith to one that is lived out in the context of the faith community.

The grid and ministry models. This grid is designed to help youth workers assess the *effectiveness* of a given youth ministry model in a particular ministry setting and to evaluates that model's theological viability. The biblical paradigm of God's reign provides the grid's theological criteria for evaluating a ministry model's effectiveness, while the developmental theories discussed in chapter 1 will be the basis for the contextual criteria. This grid can be applied to the wide variety of youth ministry models discussed earlier (page 14 and following), as long as they possess a clear vision and firmly take into account local needs and available resources.

Questions as an evaluative tool. Analytical questions will make up the primary evaluative method of this grid. These diagnostic questions are intended to be asked directly and honestly as they are applied to particular aspects of youth ministry. Faced squarely, the questions can raise awareness of both strengths and deficiencies in specific ministry areas. Collectively, these questions compose a developmental and theological grid for assessing the effectiveness and faithfulness of a youth ministry. The grid also provides key words that capture the ideal for specific areas of youth ministry.

Part 1: Evaluating Developmental Relevance

Youth ministries are most effective when they take seriously where adolescents are along the journey of individuation. As we discussed in chapter 1, the adolescent trek is extending into a fifteen-year process—maybe even longer. *Early adolescence* begins at the age of eleven or twelve. *Middle adolescence* (or midadolescence) spans the years of thirteen or fourteen to seventeen through nineteen. And *late adolescence* ends when a young person is in the mid- to late-twenties.[3] Figure 6 shows how this would look on the adolescent tightrope. To be developmentally relevant, youth ministries should be sensitive to the unique needs and issues of each stage of the adolescent journey.

Figure 6. Stages of Adolescence

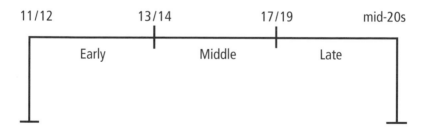

Early Adolescence. During early adolescence (junior high, grades six to eight), students still think concretely in terms of black and white. It's hard for them to see the complexities of various moral issues. Early adolescent attitudes seem schizophrenic. One moment they're on top of the world; the next moment they're in the depths of despair. Biologically they're going through a number of radical developmental changes brought on by puberty.

Early adolescents are also beginning to sense their changing role in the family and in society. They're no longer children, completely dependent on Mom or Dad. They're expected to operate more independently, often making adult-level decisions. And with elevated expectations heaped on them, they may experience an increased sense of lostness because they are not sure how to manage the changes. Since relationships seem fluid and insecure and they're not sure whom to trust, early adolescents are looking for people who make them feel safe.

In responding to this developmental level, youth ministries should pay particular attention to the ethos and environment of the ministry. At this stage, making programs feel like safe environments may be more important than ensuring that the right content is delivered. Youth ministries should focus on providing a stable and safe adult presence, with the goal of creating a sense of family. Early adolescent identity is still rooted in the family context, so they must feel the security and warmth of faith. Understanding God's unfailing love and feeling the love and acceptance of the church help to develop the warm "feel" of faith. Early adolescents also relate well to fun, active, relevant programming and teaching.

Here are a few practical ideas that can help youth ministries be more relevant during this stage. Most importantly, infuse the youth ministry with as many adults as is helpful—from a variety of ages, gifts, and interests. It's important to demonstrate to the teens that there is a wide range of adults who genuinely care for them. Have teens journal about life's struggles or faith questions in relative safety. Their adult small-group leaders can read them during the week and return them at the next meeting. In recent years, Belleview Community Church, in Littleton, Colorado, has done this with their early adolescents with surprising success.

To help youth stay connected with their family, plan a parent-teen one-day service project, watch a movie and have parents and teens talk about what they like about it, or host a parent-teen version of "The Newlywed Game." Or let students create a video version of "This is Your Life," and present it to their parents.[4]

In your teaching, use and tell stories to communicate biblical

Early adolescence: questions and key words

- In what ways is the youth ministry providing a sense of family?
- How is it focusing on the warmth and feel of faith, emphasizing acceptance, encouragement and blessing?
- To what extent are adult volunteers working to understand the journey of adolescence at this stage?
- How is the youth ministry working consistently with the students' family systems?
- How is it involving a greater numbers of mature adults?
- In what ways is the youth ministry making its program environment safe, reducing the levels of personal risk for students?
- How are leaders using the element of story to capture youths' interest and to teach truth?
- To what extent is youth ministry programming fun, energetic, and experiential?

family context—Keep a strong connection with the family.
feel of faith—At this stage this is more important than content of faith.
safety and warmth—New to the adolescent journey, early adolescents need a sense of security.
narrative—Communicate primarily through story.
energy and experience—These enhance early adolescent learning.

truth; propositional truths are often too abstract for this age and aren't usually connected to life's complexities. Adults should freely share their own life stories and teens should be given ample opportunity to tell their stories.

For this developmental stage, the following is a helpful set of evaluative questions and key words.

Middle Adolescence. During this stage (senior high, grades nine to twelve), teens are able to think more abstractly and reflect on theory. They are learning, therefore, to live with the reality of moral gray areas, and they're more able to reflect on their change of position in the family and in culture.

In middle adolescence, teenagers begin to sense adult betrayal. In response, they begin to move their world underground, away from the hostile environment of adult systems. Close peer clusters become paramount as the quest for a safe place intensifies. They're trying to survive the adult world, hoping to experience loyalty in their own world. After all, adolescents tend to be self-centered. They're pulling the locus of life's control toward themselves in order to become independent.

In response, youth ministries should strengthen the sense of community in the youth group. It is key to encourage the close relationships that develop in small groups. It's also important to continue breaking down the perceived (but not necessarily real) hostility that teens have toward adults, or might feel from them. Since teens tend to live in layers, adopting an ethic unique to each facet of their lives, teaching and discipleship must connect biblical truth with all areas of their lives: home, school, work, and extracurricular activities.

Practical ideas that correspond with this adolescent stage should focus on understanding middle adolescents, developing small groups, and rethinking adult-student relationships. Ask your adult volunteers to spend more time with the teens in relationship-driven contexts instead of limiting their involvement to content-driven settings. Adults should be spending time seeking out teens on their own turf. While that can be frightening, volunteer ministry should be primarily about going to the students.

Breaking down parent-teen barriers is important at this developmental stage. To help strengthen family bonds, host a parent-teen event. An activity called "Excuses, Excuses" can be a fun way to talk about the way parents and teenagers lean on excuses, legitimate or lame, to wiggle out of sticky situations. Present a hypothetical situation, such as, "You're a parent and you fell asleep on the couch and were late picking up your daughter after the school's talent show." After the situation is presented, give everyone one minute to write down the best excuse they can think of. Sixty seconds later, invite each one to read their excuses. Then the group votes on which excuse is the funniest and which one is the most believable. It's a great way to get teens and parents talking openly with each other about real-life situations.

In teaching, the content of faith should now become a part of the youth ministry's culture. Explore important beliefs and assumptions of Christianity and tangle with their application in life. Avoid using condescending "challenge" language, however. I have witnessed teens' faces fall when well meaning adults issue a biblical or practical challenge. That's not to say challenges can never be issued, but middle adoles-

Middle adolescence: questions and key words

- How committed is the youth ministry to breaking down adult-teen barriers?
- How well does it include a wide range of adults in terms of age, life experience, personality types, interests, and skills?
- How does the youth ministry demonstrate understanding for the middle adolescent world?
- In what ways are adult volunteers meeting teens on their own turf without a self-serving agenda?
- To what degree does the teaching encourage, invite, and persuade the students to a life of deeper faith, rather than challenging them in a way that seems condescending?
- How well does the teaching help teens practically apply biblical truth in the various layers or areas of their lives: home, school, extra curricular activities, work, and social life?
- How well does the youth ministry work with existing peer relationships in small groups, giving students opportunities to practice community?

safety and understanding—Youth programs need to foster a safe, secure environment.

encourage and invite—Present the gospel with persuasive language.

practice community—Maximize the midadolescent desire for belonging.

intimate relationships—Small groups form an effective context for community.

"going to"—Good adult-youth relationships depend on meeting youth without agenda.

practical teaching—Connect truth with all areas of life.

cents are much more open to and persuaded by invitational language.

Small groups, formed on the basis of existing peer clusters, should become the focal point of the youth ministry at this level. Discover the clusters by simply asking your students to write down the names of their best friends on an index card. After collecting the cards and carefully analyzing the results, you'll quickly find where the clusters lie. Adults play an important role in facilitating and guiding these small groups, and making sure that youth on the margins find a group. In nurturing relationships in various contexts, adults should do more asking about their students' lives, and less answering of the questions that young people are not asking. Listening without responding and holding back on instruction on specifics of how the teens' lives ought to be are key to good adult-youth relationships.

Late Adolescence. Even at this more advanced college and career age, we need to remember that young people in late adolescence are still adolescents in the sense that their quest for identity, belonging, and autonomy has not yet concluded. As they mature, however, they are moving toward interdependence. They're beginning to take responsibility for their lives, and their sense of identity is solidifying. Also, with their clusters dissolving, their sense of community is expanding. During late adolescence young people are preparing for the adult world. But they still need encouragement to make that final leap into adulthood as capable, responsible, interdependent persons in the faith community.

In response, youth ministries should emphasize mentoring relationships that integrate these young people into the faith family by encouraging them to expand the boundaries of their community beyond the cluster. Mentors can not only help late adolescents clarify their sense of identity, but also purposefully involve them in congregational life.

Here are a few practical ideas. Develop a mentoring program that connects late adolescents with growing, fully integrated adults who invest their lives in the congregation. The program should be intentional about integrating these young people into the church's life. Try using an effective spiritual gifts inventory. Have the young people take it, analyze the results, and reflect on who they are. Then connect the late adolescents with available ministries in the church. Also,

Late adolescence: questions and key words

- How is the youth ministry integrating late adolescents into the faith family?
- How well do our mentoring relationships work at this integration?
- How intentional is the youth ministry about working with church leadership to match late adolescents' gifts with valuable roles/ministries in the congregation?
- To what extent is the youth ministry helping young people expand their community beyond the cluster?
- In ways are we helping late adolescents firm up their sense of identity and autonomy?

integration—Integration into the family of faith is an important goal at this stage.

mentoring—These relationships become a primary strategy for integrating late adolescents into the church.

church-wide ministry—Involve the congregation in the ministry.

solidify identity—Now ready to enter adulthood, late adolescents need a firm sense of self.

expand community—Help late adolescents see beyond the boundaries of their peer cluster.

expand their sense of community by diversifying their small group experience. Use a variety of creative short-term small groups. These groups can be topical, or created around a specific interest or gift such as gourmet coffee, photography, or drama. These groups can connect them with a wider range of adults in the congregation.

Part 2: Evaluating Faithfulness to Kingdom Dimensions

Now it's time to integrate the theological paradigm of God's reign with the framework of today's adolescent story. This part of the grid, structured in terms of the three aspects of the contemporary adolescent narrative (identity, belonging, and autonomy as introduced in chapter 1), addresses the four kingdom dimensions (story, connecting, transforming, and future-now, as discussed in chapter 4).

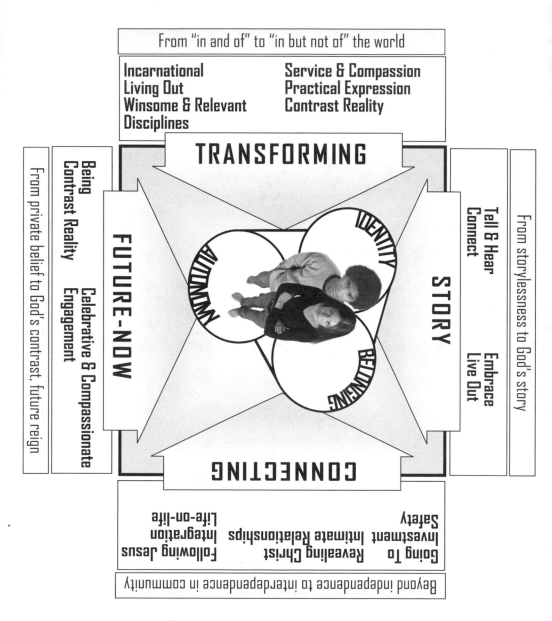

From "in and of" to "in but not of" the world

Incarnational
Living Out
Winsome & Relevant
Disciplines

Service & Compassion
Practical Expression
Contrast Reality

TRANSFORMING

Being
Contrast Reality

Celebrative & Compassionate
Engagement

FUTURE-NOW

From private belief to God's contrast, future reign

Tell & Hear
Connect

Embrace
Live Out

STORY

From storylessness to God's story

IDENTITY

COMMUNITY

BELONGING

CONNECTING

Going To

Revealing Christ

Following Jesus

Safety

Investment Intimate Relationships

Integration
Life-on-life

Beyond independence to interdependence in community

Figure 7. Evaluating Kingdom Dimensions

As each kingdom dimension is introduced, we'll review briefly the importance of the dimension, rearticulating it along with its primary goal and objectives. Then we will consider important evaluative questions. By connecting these questions to the framework of the adolescent narrative, we compose an evaluative grid. Finally, we'll identify some key words that capture the essence of each dimension. These, too, will function as a kind of road map, keeping youth ministry on course. (See figure 7 on page 136 for a compact version of the grid.)

The story dimension. The narrative of God's reign is that God has called and sent a people into the world to be a blessing to the world and to embody God's new reality. The story dimension of God's reign has an inherent tension: storylessness versus story. The primary goal in this dimension is to help adolescents make the transition from a sense of storylessness to embracing and participating in God's story of hope and blessing.

After the Exile, when the walls of Jerusalem were finally rebuilt, Ezra led the Jews in a solemn ceremony. He prayed a prayer that recounted God's faithfulness and Israel's unfaithfulness—from Abraham and Moses to that present moment (Nehemiah 9:5b-31). His prayer concluded by recognizing God's continuing mercy despite Israel's recent disobedience (32-37). Ezra and the Israelites, who had returned from captivity, now saw themselves as part of a larger, unfolding narrative. God's story was also Israel's story.

In the same way, a kingdom-driven youth ministry should give teens the opportunity to see themselves as part of God's story and the story of God's people. The objectives of the story dimension in youth ministry are: 1) to reveal to teens God's alternative story of hope and blessing; 2) to help adolescents connect to God's story throughout history; 3) to encourage them to embrace their part in God's story; and 4) to offer opportunities to live out God's story of blessing to the world.

Kingdom-driven youth ministries must winsomely and consistently connect today's teens with the mission of God's people throughout history. This means communicating the whole gospel, not just a "me-and-Jesus" message that dominates much of Christian culture and only reinforces the narratives of postmodernism and consumerism. Teens should have opportunities to reflect on their part in God's story, integrate their lives with the story of God's people, and embrace their role in it and thus discover a new sense of mission and purpose. Young people should be given outlets to practically express God's story in their world by being a blessing to others as they live out and tell the kingdom story of hope and meaning.

Practical ideas to implement the story dimension of God's reign begin with missional-focused relationships. Caring Christian adults, including emerging adults (just beyond adolescence) and more mature late adolescents, can winsomely communicate, in word and deed, that there is an alternative story to live out. On a regular basis, have adult volunteers, guests, and fellow teens share their stories of faith as a part of God's people and as participants in God's reign. Try

---

The story dimension: evaluative questions and key words

Identity	Belonging	Autonomy
• How well, and how consistently, is God's story being told? • In what ways are we helping our teens identify with God's story, and to see themselves as a part of it? • What opportunities is the youth ministry offering the students to live out God's bigger story?	• How is the youth ministry connecting teens to the story of God's people throughout history? • How well do the teens sense they're a part of God's people around the world?	• In what ways is the youth ministry helping teens realize their value as participants in God's mission for the world?

tell and hear—Liberally share God's bigger story.

connect—Consistently link the teens' story with God's story and the story of God's people.

embrace—Help adolescents own God's story.

live out—Regularly provide opportunities for young people to practice God's story in mission.

organizing a clearly focused narrative retreat where students contemplatively reflect on and identify their place in God's story. Personal mission statements can be an outcome of these retreats.

Teaching should consistently integrate God's broader kingdom narrative. Teens need a growing awareness that they are invited to receive Christ into their lives, enter God's kingdom, and participate in God's story as agents of blessing. The teaching at this level should reiterate Jesus' call to follow as an invitation to embody God's mission to the world.

Mentoring programs and small groups can guide and reinforce students' part in God's kingdom story. Shaped through careful personal and biblical reflection, these relationships can provide a context for dialogue revolving around the kingdom narrative. They can also spawn the tangible practice of being God's blessing to others.

The connecting dimension. The church is the community of God's people that embodies God's reign. In a kingdom-driven youth ministry, the connecting dimension comprises an integral method of ministry. Relationship provides the basic context for spiritual growth, faith expression, and kingdom transformation.

An inherent tension exists in this dimension—from personal and individual at one end, to communal and corporate at the other. In a kingdom-driven youth ministry, this dimension's overall goal is to move adolescents beyond individualistic independence to interdependence in the faith community. As teens develop spiritually, they grow in their understanding that they're part of Christ's body and a larger faith family (1 Corinthians 12:12-27; Matthew 12:46-48; Ephesians 4:1-5).

The specific objectives of connecting are: 1) to reach out to and develop relationships with disinterested teens in the name of Christ; 2) to invite students to have a personal relationship with Christ; 3) to offer believing students the opportunity to function and participate; 4) to deepen students' relationship with Christ in the context of close community; and 5) to incorporate students into the life of the congregation through intimate relationships with fully integrated adults.

Let's think about practical implementation. Leader-student interaction in youth ministry should always take on the form of person-to-person, incarnational relationship building. Teens need ongoing contact with a variety of caring Christian adults. For this, it is essential to look to other adults in the faith community, not just those in youth ministry leadership. Within the group itself, particularly during

The connecting dimension: evaluative questions and key words

Identity	Belonging	Autonomy
• How are we helping teenagers understand and embrace their identity as followers of Christ?	• How committed is the youth ministry to creating a safe place to explore Christ?	• How is the church validating the teens' spiritual growth as they travel on their faith journey?
• In what ways is the youth ministry using the context of community to help students shape their identity as the people of God?	• To what extent is the faith family affirming the teens as an important part of the congregation?	• What kinds of outlets are being created in which students can bless others in the congregation? • How are we helping adults receive the ministry of the teens?

going to—With missional intent, seek teens who do not yet know Christ.

investment—Building relationships with adolescents requires large amounts of effort, energy, and time.

safety—Programs and relationships must be environments in which teens feel secure.

revealing Christ—Lift up Christ in a way that engages the heart, mind, and imagination.

following Jesus—Emphasize discipleship as a lifelong journey with Jesus.

intimate relationships—Close relationships developed in small groups is a way to express faith.

integration—Continually move toward incorporating adolescents into the life of the church.

life-on-life—Understand adult-teen relationships in terms of lifelong mentoring and modeling.

the middle adolescent years, it is in peer-centered small groups that the youth will find prime connections. In the latter settings, adults function less as leaders and more as guides who facilitate Christian community.

Teaching should focus on the gospel narratives, especially Jesus' encounters with his disciples, the crowds, and opponents. Here, it is important to tell the biblical stories from fresh perspectives to capture students' imagination. The youth group environment should be sufficiently safe for students to ask hard life and faith questions. The teaching itself should highlight communal expressions of faith, promoting the church as a faith family, the tangible expression of Christ's body.

It is in this dimension that corporate prayer, worship, and community life come into play. Emphasize and develop spiritual gifts and offer outlets to practice service. Provide a living laboratory for students to bear each others' burdens and forgive one another. Students must see faith as not only "me and Jesus," but "me and Jesus in the context of relationships."

Effective programs in the connecting dimension include typical youth ministry activities, such as midweek meetings, retreats, camps, conferences, and outreach events. Make every effort, however, to practice community in focused Bible study, corporate worship, and prayer. Small groups, especially central during the high school years, can be retooled to focus more on fleshing out faith in community than on curriculum content. To do this, adults will loosen their grip on the teaching reigns to some extent. They can allow the teens to direct more of the small group content and activity.

The transforming dimension. Entering God's reign begins with individual change and continues with ever deeper levels of personal growth. Eventually, young people come to a place in which they participate in transforming the kingdom of this world into the reign of Christ. The transformational tension in God's kingdom is the movement beyond personal transformation to societal change. The primary goal in the transforming dimension of a kingdom-driven youth ministry is to move young people from being "in and of" the world to being "in but not of" the world while also "not out of" the world. Like the man who declared, "I was blind, but now I see" (John 9:25), teens can experience change on a personal level. But the transforming nature of Christ also extends to the world around them. Their collective witness makes a difference too. Remember how the first church in Jerusalem fleshed out God's new reality? Their witness attracted new believers to their fellowship each day (Acts 2:42-47) and began turning the world upside down (Acts 17:6-7).

The primary objectives of this dimension are: 1) to influence young people through our lives, inviting them to consider the life-transforming decision to trust and follow Christ; 2) to persuasively present the good news of Christ and his kingdom, encouraging teens to enter God's reign; 3) to help early and middle adolescents develop spiritual disciplines of Bible study, prayer, and worship; 4) to offer middle and late adolescents opportunities to follow Jesus in practicing service and compassion; and 5) to empower late adolescents and emerging adults to transform their world by showing others the celebrative, compassionate contrast culture of the kingdom.

To help youth practice the transforming dimension, mission-minded Christians (adults, even late adolescents) need to invest heavy doses of time and energy into the lives of teens, especially those who have made no commitment to Christ. This means youth workers will model the freedom and joy of the transformation that Jesus has made in their own lives. Adults must see themselves as those who come alongside, offering opportunities in small groups to serve each other within the group and those outside it. Mentoring relationships should follow a life-on-life approach to faith development.

The teaching of youth should present the gospel as *both* personal salvation *and* entrance into God's kingdom. It should emphasize a process of ongoing discipleship that is fed by individual spiritual practices and disciplines. Reiterate the conviction and paradox that faith in Christ can only be developed by obeying Christ, even while obedience flows out of knowing and trusting in Christ. Teaching should emphasize Jesus' ministry and instruction, especially the Sermon on the Mount—the catechism of Christ. As adolescents mature, take advantage of teachable moments. Use small group times to take teens off-site to do service or to learn about the world into which God calls them. Students, with their mentors, can model and

The transforming dimension: evaluative questions and key words

Identity

- In what ways is the youth ministry communicating to young people that, as they follow Jesus, their identity is also being transformed into his image?
- How is it using spiritual disciplines to reshape students' sense of self?
- How does it help teens see themselves as change agents in their world?

Belonging

- How consistently does the youth ministry communicate to teens that entering God's reign means both personal change and belonging to a people that is transforming the world?
- How are intimate relationships in community affecting spiritual growth?
- What opportunities are being provided for students to be a tangible, contrast culture?

Autonomy

- How is the church validating the teens' spiritual growth as they travel on their faith journey?
- What kinds of outlets are being created in which students can bless others in the congregation?
- How are we helping adults receive the ministry of the teens?

incarnational—Adults must move toward the world of teens, developing genuine relationships.

living out—Volunteers should embody the authentic transformation of Jesus.

winsome and relevant—The life- and world-changing gospel of Christ must be persuasively presented effectively.

disciplines—Spiritual disciplines effect spiritual change in adolescents.

service and compassion—These are primary methods of kingdom change.

practical expression—Consistently provide outlets for students to embody the kingdom.

contrast reality—Help teens grasp their role in a tangible counternarrative.

lead others in countercultural acts of justice, righteousness, service, compassion, and community.

In this transforming dimension, camps, conventions, and retreats may be the most efficient program context for accomplishing the objectives of kingdom change. Find ways to introduce and develop spiritual disciplines that help create a deeper bond with Jesus. The most powerful program response may be involvement in mission trips and service projects. Such activities give adolescents at all developmental stages opportunities to live out, model, and effect change in their world.

The future-now dimension. This area of a kingdom-driven youth ministry asks us to consider what it means to model an alternative culture before a watching world. Participating in God's reign means wrapping our arms around the idea that a local church and its youth ministry are called to be a sign of God's coming new order—a world in which God rules. The main focus of this dimension is on the way the church interacts with the world. It takes seriously the question, "What does it mean to participate in compassionate, selfless social justice in the context of a faith community?"

The tension here has to do with private belief and contrast-cultural living. The overall goal of the future-now dimension is to move adolescents from holding to a faith composed only of private belief to one that expresses and embodies the contrast culture of God's future reign. Jesus continually called his hearers to express a kingdom reality (Matthew 5:1-20; Mark 10:13-16; Luke 18:18-29). Paul too urged his readers to practice contrast-kingdom living (Romans 12:1-21; 14:17-18; Ephesians 5:4-5). And this call extends to us today. In the midst of our world, we are called to embody a parallel, alternative reality. By being *parallel* we never stop relating to those around us. And by being *alternative* we continually demonstrate a competing reality.[5] And we live out this tension, anticipating God's ultimate reign when "the kingdom of the world has become the kingdom of our Lord and of his Messiah" (Revelation 11:15).

The main objectives of this dimension reflect the witness of the youth ministry as a whole: 1) to be a growing community of passionate, journey-conscious followers of Christ; 2) to embody a celebrative, contrast culture of generosity, justice, and compassion; and 3) to model God's reign in such a way that others are drawn to participate.

This dimension of youth ministry expresses and extends all the other kingdom dimensions, providing a theological guide for engaging our world. As an eschatological sign of God's future reign, the youth ministry lives out God's narrative of hope and blessing, connecting in authentic community, being transformed into God's people, and expressing a contrast culture of justice and compassion in the world. Through all of these commitments, the youth are part of the church's mission to show humanity God's future world.

Practical ideas for nurturing the future-now dimension of youth ministry ought to include activities that facilitate the task of cultural engagement through a balance of action and reflection. Give students, especially late adolescents, numerous guided opportunities for such engagement. These could be mission trips, service projects, or youth events that use as ministry springboards such culturally symbolic events as the Super Bowl, the Stanley Cup finals, or the DVD release of a blockbuster movie. While these are common youth ministry activities, what's often missing is the careful reflection that should follow these events. Use post-event debriefing sessions as opportunities for students to reflect on how they interact with their world. Among other questions, ask students: "What was easy about your encounter? What was difficult? What surprised you? How did you see God working? What skills did your interaction demand? How did you reveal God's kingdom? How was it received?"

As a youth group (or as a smaller group), do an *Anknupfungspunkt*— German for "the point of buttoning on." Select a cultural artifact or icon that, in some ways, expresses an aspect of the culture's narrative—a movie, a song, an advertising slogan, or a sporting event. Then examine ways in which this artifact could become a means for a fresh encounter of the good news of Christ. In other words, how can it be a point of "buttoning on" the gospel?

Consider helping more mature students write personal mission statements, encouraging them to find ways to reflect God's story in their own story; or, as an ongoing project, provide the basic framework for students to recite their personal salvation history.[6] Such a

**The future-now dimension:
evaluative questions and key words**

Identity	Belonging	Autonomy
• How is the youth ministry ascertaining that the teens' sense of identity is clearly defined and durable? • How is it consistently creating opportunities for cultural engagement that sharpen the students' identity as kingdom seekers?	• How can the ministry facilitate a sense of belonging as adolescents corporately express God's contrast vision?	• In what ways is the youth ministry integrating student participation in God's mission/call with the students' growing sense of value and purpose?

being—Students, and the entire youth ministry, personify God's reign.

contrast reality—Corporate expression of the kingdom is both spiritual and tangible.

celebrative and compassionate—These are marks of the kingdom's contrast community.

engagement—Being in, but not of, the world brings into focus the meaning of discipleship.

project integrates God's story as revealed in Scripture with their story and their part in God's mission for the world.

Discipleship, Encounter, Outreach (DEO) is an initiative of Mennonite Mission Network that effectively develops this dimension. Targeted to people ages eighteen to thirty, DEO is designed to be an adventure in which young adults can find themselves, serve others, and discover God on the journey of discipleship. The year-long program consists of three phases: discipleship training, service encounters in a cross-cultural setting, and ministry internships in the participants' home congregations. Through DEO's holistic approach, participants live out the future-now dimension of youth ministry. While most local congregations may not have the resources to reproduce a program like this, any youth ministry program can adapt the kind of eschatological focus that the program embodies.[7]

Being the visible expression of God's kingdom counternarrative ought to be the end result of a youth ministry's teaching, programs, activities, and relationships. The overall movement of a kingdom-driven youth ministry should reflect a continual growth toward being agents of God's reign in the world, embodying authentic community and living celebratively as a people of compassion. Such a radical worldview engages the world by modeling a new reality with a clear invitation to participate.

Developmental Outcomes

Thus far, we have outlined how the paradigm of God's reign can raise evaluative issues for youth ministry. Now, however, it is important to reconnect the kingdom dimensions with basic developmental objectives. So let us briefly describe ways in which the reign of God correlates with the stages of early, middle, and late adolescence. If your youth ministry is shaped by God's kingdom, you may notice your teens achieving certain observable outcomes. We recognize, of course, that teenage spiritual growth rarely happens on "schedule," and that some are ready to develop much sooner than others. What follows, therefore, is not a formula to be applied to every situation; it describes the ideal. But if you are seeing a few of these outcomes happening, be encouraged.

Outcomes of the story dimension. Kingdom-driven youth ministries attempt to move teens from a sense of storylessness to embracing God's story of blessing for the world. Developmentally, *early and middle adolescents* will find themselves connecting their individual story with God's story throughout Scripture and history. They will begin to realize that God has called them, too, sending them to be a blessing in their world. Building on their connection to God's story, middle adolescents will be able to articulate and move toward embracing their part in God's story. You may hear them share it freely in conversations with friends or interested adults. They will own their role as participants in God's kingdom purposes. *Late adolescents* will take advantage of real-life opportunities to be God's story of blessing to the world. They may seek out opportunities to be a blessing through acts of compassion, justice, and generosity, and encourage others to participate with them.

Outcomes of the connecting dimension. In the relational dimension, a kingdom-driven youth ministry seeks to move adolescents from self-focused individualism to interdependence in community. *Early adolescents* in the youth ministry will begin to relate to Christ on a personal level; they will be drawn to Jesus in a way that engages their hearts and minds. You might observe them praying spontaneously, hear about insights they discover in their Bible reading, or find them emotionally moved during worship music. Both *early and middle adolescents* will feel free to function in community at an introductory level, eagerly participating in corporate prayer, worship, and Bible study groups.

Middle adolescents will begin to see their faith as a relationship with Christ within the context of close community. Drawing on their desire for peer relationships, they will contribute to a more intimate communal experience of faith. For example, they might set up an Internet-use accountability group as a way of coping with online temptations. Or they may arrange clandestine prayer meetings at school in a coordinated effort to pray for a friend to encounter Christ. *Late adolescents* will begin to see themselves as full participants in the faith community, incorporated into its structure and life. They may, for example, volunteer to coordinate the nursery schedule or to work in the church kitchen. They may even be eager to serve on the finance committee.

Outcomes of the transforming dimension. This kingdom dimension moves adolescents from being in and of the world to being followers of Jesus who are in but not of the world (but not out of the world, either). *Early adolescents* will be able to clearly understand the life-transforming good news of Christ and his kingdom. They will grasp the personal change that comes as they enter God's reign and begin following Christ. You may notice their language is more encouraging, they make wiser movie choices, and their actions are more others-centered. *Middle adolescents* will begin to deepen their faith by developing devotional disciplines such as Bible study, prayer, and worship. For instance, they may begin asking you some perceptive questions about Bible passages that indicate they're moving deeper spiritually.

Late adolescents will begin integrating their discipleship with their lifestyle and vocational decisions. They will become more self-giving, looking for ways to practice acts of service and compassion. As they emerge into adulthood, they will be better able to understand how they can transform their world by showing those around them the contrast culture of God's reign. You might discover, for example, that their Sunday school class has initiated a regular movie discussion group that meets at a coffee shop next to the local theater. As they muse about the movie's characters and storyline, their respectful, humble dialogue reflects and models a curiously contrasting worldview.

Outcomes of the future-now dimension. A kingdom-driven youth ministry desires to move young people from a faith of private belief to one that embodies the contrast culture of God's future reign. This future-now dimension works toward collective outcomes, where the youth ministry itself expresses something of God's coming kingdom. Individual students, however, make up the collective expression, and must be nurtured toward the vision both individually and corporately. The ultimate goal is that by the time young people are *late adolescents*—on the cusp of adulthood—they will demonstrate, before a watching world, a growing community of passionate, journey-conscious followers of Christ that live out a celebrative contrast culture. They do this in such a way that others are drawn to participate in God's reign, too.

The ultimate desire of a kingdom-driven youth ministry is that, along the way, adolescents (*early, middle,* and *late*) progressively and ever-more fully demonstrate the future-now (eschatological) dimension of God's reign. This is accomplished *narratively* as teens move toward embracing and living out God's story of hope and blessing. It is achieved *relationally* as they grow as interdependent members of the faith community. It is also realized *transformationally* as adolescents move beyond personal change to being participants in broader societal renovation.

Conclusion

In essence, a kingdom-driven youth ministry is about "whole gospel and whole life." It integrates a large theology that addresses the complexities and mysteries of life. Taking the Kingdom-Driven Youth Ministry Grid seriously can help youth leaders extend popular youth ministry models so that they integrate broader aspects of the gospel and life. For example, the purpose-driven youth ministry model actively works to move teens toward a deeper personal relationship with Christ. Along the way, however, a disconnect with the larger church family often seems to develop.[8] As a guide for youth ministry, the paradigm of God's kingdom and its connecting (relational) dimension can help a purpose-driven youth ministry to more creatively integrate teens into the larger faith community.

Our paradigm also offers a corrective to the family-based youth ministry movement. It works hard to integrate young people into the life of the church family, which is an admirable goal. However, it offers no clear indication that these teens have a strong understanding of God's story of blessing to the world, much less a coherent grasp of their role in that narrative. The story (narrative) dimension of a kingdom-driven youth ministry could help family-based youth ministries move teens toward embracing and living out God's narrative of blessing and hope to the world outside the faith community.

The ministry model set forth in Kenda Creasy Dean and Ron Foster's important work, *The Godbearing Life*, calls for youth ministries to develop teens as Godbearers to others in the context of community. They clearly emphasize community in spiritual development, but the practical outworking of faith is limited to the personal sphere of one's life. Their focus seems to be on individuals who have been personally changed, working toward the personal transformation of others. All of this reflects a common understanding of salvation, but the gospel transcends personal transformation. The reign of God's future-now (eschatological) dimension can help move teens toward nurturing their faith community to be a contrast culture in the midst of the world.

Tony Jones' widely read book, *Postmodern Youth Ministry*, urges youth ministers to take seriously our current postmodern cultural context. Its call is for youth ministry to be missional in its approach, contextualizing the gospel for a new generation. But what is lost in the midst of Jones' call to be "in the world" is a clear understanding of authentic transformation. While we are in the world contextualizing the gospel, how do we work at being a contrast culture that is not "of the world" but nevertheless influences the world? The transforming and future-now dimensions of God's reign can help teens and youth ministries follow a kingdom transformation strategy, changing the world by showing the world the beauty of God's reign.

The kingdom of God is a biblical narrative that effectively engages the contemporary adolescent narrative. It can also function as a powerful theological paradigm for guiding youth ministry practice in today's teenage world. Kingdom-driven youth leaders see God's reign as their foundational, sweeping, and dynamic biblical paradigm for youth ministry. From a kingdom perspective, they are grounded in a clear understanding of adolescent development, meeting teens at their point of spiritual commitment. In their programming, kingdom-driven youth ministries integrate all four dimensions of God's reign: story, connecting, transforming, and future-now. They seek to help teens become fully-devoted followers of Jesus who are integrated into the larger family of faith—young people who embody and participate in the contrast culture of God's reign. In the end, kingdom-driven youth ministries weave together whole gospel and whole life.

This generation needs the whole gospel to be boldly lived out in such a way that people can see it, touch it, and know that it's real. Imagine the influence of a generation of kingdom-driven young women and men who are willing to follow Jesus daily, radically, and totally in life. The kingdom-driven youth ministry grid offered here seeks to provide a deep theological framework for realizing such a dream, a framework that offers teens a more compelling narrative than the one their culture instills in them. Those of us in youth ministry have an opportunity to participate with God in raising up a new generation of Christian leaders with a deep desire to reshape the world. May we be faithful in embracing that opportunity today.

Postlude

Running Alongside
Ministry *With*: God, People, Place

Over the last two decades, my youth ministry experience has been tainted by the struggle of loving the idea of youth ministry more than the young people for whom I'm called to care. As many youth workers know, the priorities of paying attention to God and ministering to teens can easily fall by the wayside. Over time, I've witnessed youth ministry in general become something of an industry. We've become enamored with flash, technique, and style. Hot worship bands, high-energy, enormous youth events, and high profile programs have replaced the essence of faithful ministry: incarnational relationships. Much of youth ministry seems to reflect adult-driven agendas. It's about making us adult leaders look good and not about pouring ourselves into the lives of adolescents. I wonder if youth ministry has become more about us as youth workers than anything else.

In recent years, my time spent immersed in teen culture and researching adolescence itself has helped me refocus on what ministry is all about: helping youth in a particular place pay attention to God. It's not about me. It's about God and the teens. It's a holy convergence of mystery (God) and mess (us).[1] I have realized that I need to rediscover the heart of youth ministry. Maybe we all do.

One spring, I had an experience that brought this into sharp focus for me. Between classes one day, I slipped out of the office to watch my son Taylor run the 50-meter dash. It was one of those grade school track and field days in which everyone gets to compete whether they want to or not. And I had to pay attention. The 50-meter dash is short enough that if another parent called my name, I might turn around and miss it.

Just before Taylor's race was the fifth-grade boys' 1600-meter run. That's four times around the track—about a mile—which is a long way for anyone, much less a boy in grade five. As the runners gathered at the starting line, I noticed Gabe. No one really liked Gabe. He was a bully. Since he was short, round, and non-athletic, I knew there was no way Gabe was going to win the race. I'm sure he didn't train for the event. He may not even have known what the event really demanded. "Four times around the track?" he sneered in his childhood naiveté. "Is that all? Sure I can do it."

The gun went off, and within seconds the other competitors bolted ahead of Gabe, bounding like gazelles—just as I expected. But Gabe, with his head down, shuffled along. After two laps, Gabe had been overtaken. The other four boys soon crossed the finish line. Their parents, video cameras in hand, were congratulating and hugging their child prodigies.

But Gabe was still on the track, only on his third lap. As he shuffled around the second turn, coming to the home stretch, Gabe's head was still down. He was pouring sweat, his face red with exhaustion and embarrassment. I thought to myself, "Just step off the track. Save yourself the humiliation." But to his credit, Gabe kept running.

The bell sounded to signal the final lap. Gabe was still shuffling. I cringed. This was going to be a while. But as Gabe started on the last lap, one of the teachers shot across the infield to intercept him. "Finally," I thought, "she'll spare him the embarrassment and get him off the track so the meet can stay on schedule." But when she reached him, the teacher hopped on the track and started running with him.

I could see that she was talking to him. I'm not sure what she said, but I guessed it was something like, "It doesn't matter what everyone else thinks. You can do it. I know you can, because we'll do it together."

As the two rounded the final turn and entered the home stretch, the teacher slowed down and stepped out of Gabe's view. She turned to the crowd and urged all of us to stand and cheer Gabe on. Slowly, one by one, the students, teachers, and parents rose to their feet applauding. We chanted, "Gabe, Gabe, Gabe." With a short burst of speed Gabe crossed the finish line. His face was beaming with triumph and joy.

To this day I can't remember who won that race, but I'll never forget Gabe. Nor will I forget the teacher who ran alongside. That was perhaps the greatest moment of humanity I'd ever witnessed. It was a kingdom moment.

What happened that day captures some important ministry values. First, the teacher modeled Christ's kingdom ethics of love for the outcast and the marginalized. It was a flash of upside-down, kingdom brilliance—a window into God's future reign. It was a window into how Christ's kingdom invitation inspires and transforms not only our lives but also our world.

Second, the teacher exemplified an essential reorientation to youth ministry. So many adolescents feel like they're running on the track of life alone. No adults are on the track and few really care. For the sake of an emerging generation and for the sake of God's kingdom, it's time that we adults abandon our self-focused, adult-driven agendas and recommit to what really matters: life-on-life youth ministry.

It's time we come out of our seats and get on the track with our teens. It's time we demonstrate a counterculture where adults are integrally involved in the lives of youth. We need to surround our teens with a scaffold of faith and community. That support structure will not only steady them on the journey of adolescence; it will help them frame a viable life story that gives them meaning and hope.

Notes

Introduction

1. Many of the stories in this book are based on actual events. Others, like this one, are scenarios developed out of and rooted in genuine experiences.

2. Mike Yaconelli, "The Failure of Youth Ministry," *Youthworker* 20 (May/June 2003): 64.

3. Pete Ward, in *God at the Mall: Youth Ministry that Meets Kids Where They're At* (Peabody, MA: Hendrickson, 1999). Tony Jones, in *Postmodern Youth Ministry: Exploring Cultural Shift, Creating Holistic Connections, Cultivating Authentic Community* (Grand Rapids, MI: Zondervan, 2001). See Mark DeVries, *Family-Based Youth Ministry: Revised and Expanded* 2d ed. (Downers Grove, IL: InterVarsity Press, 2004). Kenda Creasy Dean and Ron Foster, *The Godbearing Life: The Art of Soul Tending for Youth Ministry* (Nashville, TN: Upper Room Books, 1998).

4. Mark Senter III first raised this issue in his book, *The Coming Revolution in Youth Ministry and Its Radical Impact on the Church* (Wheaton, IL: Victor Books, 1992), 139-52. The trend has only increased in recent years.

5. Chap Clark, "The Changing Face of Adolescence: A Theological View of Human Development," in *Starting Right: Thinking Theologically about Youth Ministry*, eds. Kenda Creasy Dean, Chap Clark, and Dave Rahn (Grand Rapids, MI: Zondervan, 2001), 42.

6. Kenda Creasy Dean, "Theological Rocks—First Things First," in *Starting Right: Thinking Theologically about Youth Ministry*, 19.

7. In this discussion, the term "model" refers to any conceptual framework that articulates the structure, strategies, and goals of youth ministry.

8. This emphasis has continued to gain momentum since the late 1980s.

9. See Chap Clark, "The Myth of the Perfect Youth Ministry Model," in *Starting Right*, 110-11.

10. Mark H. Senter III, "Youth Programs," in *Youth Education in the Church*, eds. Roy B. Zuck, and Warren S. Benson (Chicago, IL: Moody Press, 1978), 267-83.

11. Senter, "Basic Models of Youth Ministry," in *The Coming Revolution in Youth Ministry*, 164.

12. Duffy Robbins, *This Way to Youth Ministry: An Introduction to the Adventure* (Grand Rapids, MI: Zondervan, 2004), 500-12. Here Robbins

builds upon his funnel model which he first advocated in *Youth Ministry that Works* (Wheaton, IL: Victor Books, 1991), 80. This funnel, which can be inverted into a pyramid, focuses ministry around six levels of spiritual commitment. The "Pool of Humanity" represents the teen population within a given geographical location. At this level the youth ministry reaches out to the masses. The "Come Level" targets teens that do not yet have a relationship with Christ, but attend ministry events. The goal here is to get these youth to come to Christ. The "Grow Level" is designed for students that have made an initial commitment to Jesus. The hope is to help them grow in their faith. The "Disciple Level" of the ministry reaches the teens who take initiative for their own spiritual growth. This level is designed to help these young people mature as disciples. The "Develop Level" targets students who demonstrate a burden for their friends' spiritual growth. The goal is to develop them as leaders. Finally, the "Multiplier Level" equips and empowers spiritually mature students to reproduce themselves, to be disciplers.

13. Sonlife Ministries, *Strategy: Growing a Healthy Youth Ministry: The Strategy of Jesus* (Chicago, IL: Sonlife Ministries, 1999).

14. Doug Fields, *Purpose Driven Youth Ministry: 9 Essential Foundations for Healthy Growth* (Grand Rapids, MI: Zondervan, 1998).

15. J.R.R. Tolkien, *The Fellowship of the Ring: Being the First Part of The Lord of the Rings*, 2d ed. (Boston, MA: Houghton Mifflin Company, 1987), 60.

16. Fields, *Purpose Driven Youth Ministry*, 43-54.

17. Ray S. Anderson, *The Soul of Ministry: Forming Leaders for God's People*, (Louisville, KY: Westminster John Knox Press, 1997), 17-24.

Chapter One

1. Chap Clark, *Hurt: Inside the World of Today's Teenagers* (Grand Rapids, MI: Baker Academic, 2004), 28. See also, Chap Clark, "The Changing Face of Adolescence," in *Starting Right: Thinking Theologically about Youth Ministry*. eds. Kenda Creasy Dean, Chap Clark, and Dave Rahn (Grand Rapids, MI: Zondervan, 2001), 45-47.

2. Clark, "The Changing Face of Adolescence," 50.

3. Clark, *Hurt*, 28-29.

4. Patricia Hersch's influential study, *A Tribe Apart: A Journey into the Heart of American Adolescence* (New York, NY: Ballantine Books, 1999), and Chap Clark's *Hurt: Inside the World of Today's Teenagers* both emphasize the damaging effects of undue adult pressures.

5. Ron Powers, "The Apocalypse of Adolescence," Atlantic Monthly 289 (March 2002): par. 76. Database online. Available from FirstSearch, <http://newfirstsearch.oclc.org.> Accessed [22 July 2003].

6. See Clark, *Hurt*, 39-56.

7. Clark, *Hurt*, 44.

8. According to Mintel, a market research group, teens from twelve to seventeen years of age were estimated to have spent over $153 billion in 2006.

9. Steve Wulf, "Generation Excluded," Time, 23 October 1995, 86.

10. See Mike A. Males' works, *Framing Youth: 10 Myths about the Next Generation* (Monroe, ME: Common Courage Press, 1999); *The Scapegoat Generation: America's War on Adolescents* (Monroe, ME: Common Courage Press, 1996), "The True 'Greatest Generation' of our Time: X," Los Angeles Times, 26 April 2001; <http://home.earthlink.net/-mmales/genx.html.> [16 July 2003].

11. This is basis of Clark's book *Hurt: Inside the World of Today's Teenagers*. See also, Patricia Hersch, *A Tribe Apart: A Journey into the Heart of American Adolescence*.

12. David Elkind, *Ties That Stress: The New Family Imbalance* (Cambridge, MA: Harvard University Press, 1994), 188-208. Adolescent psychologist David Elkind has written extensively on implications of changing family systems on teens and children. Three of his books are worth reading on this. *Ties That Stress*; *The Hurried Child: Growing Up Too Fast Too Soon*, 3d ed. (Cambridge, MA: Perseus Books), 2001; and *All Grown Up and No Place to Go* (Reading, MA: Addison-Wesley), 1998.

13. For further reading, see Mark DeVries, *Family-Based Youth Ministry*, Revised and Expanded, 2d ed. (Downers Grove, IL: InterVarsity Press, 2004), 36-43.

14. For a more complete summary, see Clark, *Hurt*, 7-13, and Chapman R. Clark, "Entering Their World: A Qualitative Look at the Changing Face of Contemporary Adolescence," *Journal of Youth Ministry* (Fall 2002), 9-21.

15. See Fred Engh's book, *Why Johnny Hates Sports: Why Organized Youth Sports Are Failing Our Children and What We Can Do About It* (Garden City Park, NY: Square One Publishers, 2002).

16. Clark, *Hurt*, 43.

17. This term has been made popular by Neil Howe, William Strauss, and R. J. Matson in their book, *Millennials Rising: The Next Great Generation* (New York, NY: Vintage, 2000).

18. This is an educated guess at best. It would be interesting to see the results of future studies on the behavioral outcomes of children of helicopter parents.

19. See Clark, *Hurt*, 136-44.

20. "Caught Cheating," an ABC "Primetime" special was aired on April 29, 2004. The special explored the growing level of cheating by students. In a six-month investigation, "Primetime" visited colleges and high schools across America to discover how today's students cheat and to look at the possible reasons they do it. The overwhelming reason for cheating that students gave was "pressure" from teachers and parents. See also Clark, *Hurt*, 149-56.

21. Clark, "The Changing Face of Adolescence," 53.

22. Clark, "The Changing Face of Adolescence," 56.

23. Donald Posterski was the first to use the term cluster to identify these close-knight friendship groups. See *Friendship: A Window on Ministry to Youth* (Scarborough, ON: Project Teen Canada, 1985), 8.

24. See, Chap Clark, *Hurt*, 78-85.

25. For more on the world beneath, see Clark, *Hurt*, 87-165.

26. David Elkind identifies this scaffold as an envelope against which teens push. See, *A Sympathetic Understanding of the Child: Birth to Sixteen* (Needham Heights, MA: Allyn and Bacon, 1994), 203.

27. C. Norman Kraus, *Community of the Spirit: How the Church Is in the World*, rev. ed. (Scottdale, PA: Herald Press, 1992), 28.

Chapter Two

1. Leonard Sweet, *SoulTsunami: Sink or Swim in New Millennium Culture* (Grand Rapids, MI: Zondervan, 1999), 17.

2. Douglas Groothius, *Truth Decay: Defending Christianity against the Challenges of Postmodernism* (Downers Grove, IL: InterVarsity Press, 2000), 11.

3. Stanley J. Grenz, *A Primer on Postmodernism* (Grand Rapids: William B. Eerdmans Publishing Company, 1996), 2.

4. James K. A. Smith, *Who's Afraid of Postmodernism?: Taking Derrida, Lyotard and Foucault to Church* (Grand Rapids, MI: Baker Academic, 2006), 64.

5. Smith, *Who's Afraid of Postmodernism?*, 62.

6. J. Richard Middleton and Brian J. Walsh, *Truth Is Stranger Than It Used to Be: Biblical Faith in a Postmodern Age* (Downers Grove, IL: InterVarsity Press, 1995), 34.

7. Sweet, *SoulTsunami*, 28.

8. Tony Jones, *Postmodern Youth Ministry: Exploring Cultural Shift, Creating Holistic Connections, Cultivating Authentic Community* (Grand Rapids, MI: Zondervan, 2001), 34.

9. Christian Smith, *Soul Searching: The Religious and Spiritual Lives of American Teenagers* (New York, NY: Oxford University Press, 2005), 72-117.

10. Stanley J. Grenz, *Created for Community: Connecting Christian Belief with Christian Living*, 2d ed. (Grand Rapids, MI: Baker Books, 1998), 214.

Chapter Three

1. William D. Romanowski, *Eyes Wide Open: Looking for God in Popular Culture* (Grand Rapids, MI: Baker Book House, 2001), 42.

2. Quentin J. Schultze, "How Should We Respond to Popular Culture?" in *Reaching a Generation for Christ*, eds. Richard R. Dunn and Mark H. Senter III, 439-53 (Chicago, IL: Moody Press, 1997), 441.

3. Michael Budde, *The (Magic) Kingdom of God* (Boulder, CO: Westview Press, 1997), 14.

4. Budde, *The (Magic) Kingdom of God*, 27.

5. Richard T. Hughes, *Myths America Lives By* (Urbana, IL: University of Illinois Press), 149.

6. In her book, *No Logo: Taking Aim at the Brand Bullies* (New York,

NY: Picado, 1999), Naomi Klein is critical of marketing's effects on culture. In a *PBS/Frontline* interview, she discusses the influence of branding. http://www.pbs.org/wgbh/pages/frontline/shows/persuaders/interviews/klein.html. [Accessed, May 10, 2007].

7. Howard Schultz, *Pour Yourself into It* (New York, NY: Hyperion, 1997), 5, quoted in Naomi Klein, No Logo, 20.

8. The *60 Minutes* episode aired April 23, 2006.

9. iTunes.com was accessed July, 2006.

10. Apple reported shipping over 14 million iPods in the first quarter of 2006 alone.

11. Douglas Rushkoff spends a lot of time developing these two media caricatures in his *Frontline* documentary, "The Merchants of Cool."

12. mountaindew.com was accessed July, 2006.

13. "Merchants of Cool: Tour This Landscape."

14. Dee Dee Gordon and Sharon Lee of Look-Look, and Irma Zandl of The Zandl Group are considered some of the leaders in the business of cool hunting.

Chapter Four

1. In this book I'll use the words "reign" and "kingdom" of God interchangeably—for stylistic reasons (occasionally using "empire" or "dominion"). The term "kingdom of God" has a long, rich theological and scholarly tradition. I prefer to use the term "reign of God" because it has greater gender inclusiveness for contemporary readers.

2. For further study on the reign of God, see John Bright's classic, and still relevant, work, *The Kingdom of God: The Biblical Concept and Its Meaning for the Church* (New York: NY: Abingdon-Cokesbury Press, 1953). A recent book that develops God's reign is Brian McLaren's, *The Secret Message of Jesus: Uncovering the Truth that Could Change Everything* (Nashville, TN: W Publishing Group, 2006).

3. Donald B. Kraybill, *The Upside-Down Kingdom* (Scottdale, PA: Herald Press, 1990), 19.

4. Kraybill, *The Upside-Down Kingdom*, 20.

5. N. T. Wright, *The Challenge of Jesus: Rediscovering Who Jesus Was and Is* (Downers Grove, IL: InterVarsity Press, 1999), 47.

6. Ulrich Becker, "*euangélion*," *New International Dictionary of New Testament Theology*, vol. 2, ed. Colin Brown. (Grand Rapids, MI: Zondervan, 1986), 112.

7. Darrell L. Guder, *Missional Church: A Vision for Sending of the Church in North America* (Grand Rapids, MI: Eerdmans, 1998), 88.

8. Rodney Clapp, *A Peculiar People: The Church as Culture in a Post-Christian World* (Downers Grove, IL: InterVarsity Press, 1996), 78.

9. N. T. Wright, *The New Testament and the People of God* (Minneapolis, MN: Fortress, 1992), 169.

10. Kraybill discusses this event at length in *The Upside-Down Kingdom*, 35-88. This brief discussion is taken primarily from his work. See also, Matthew 4:1-11; Luke 4:1-13.

11. Joel B. Green, *The Way of the Cross* (Nashville, TN: Discipleship Resources, 1991), 70.

12. Myron S. Augsburger, *The Robe of God* (Scottdale, PA: Herald Press, 2000), 88.

13. Augsburger, *The Robe of God*, 87.

14. Wilbert R. Shenk, *Write the Vision: The Church Renewed* (Valley Forge, PA: Trinity Press International, 1995), 94.

15. Guder, *Missional Church*, 86.

16. See Guder, *Missional Church*, 93-109.

17. Augsburger, *The Robe of God*, 78-79.

18. Stanley Hauerwas and William H. Willimon, *Resident Aliens* (Nashville, TN: Abingdon Press, 1989), 46.

19. The concept of "polarities" or "tension points" in the kingdom of God comes from Howard A. Snyder, *Models of the Kingdom* (Nashville, TN: Abingdon Press, 1991), 16-19. Snyder identifies six polarities of God's reign: 1) present versus future; 2) individual versus social; 3) spirit versus matter; 4) gradual versus climactic; 5) divine action versus human action; and 6) the church's relation to the kingdom.

20. James Brownson, Inagrace T. Dietterich, Barry A. Harvey, and Charles C. West, *Stormfront: The Good News of God* (Grand Rapids, MI: William B. Eerdmans Publishing Company, 2003), vi-xii.

21. Brownson, et al, *Stormfront*, 108.

22. Guder, *Missional Church*, 97.

23. John Howard Yoder, "Why Ecclesiology Is Social Ethics: Gospel Ethics Versus the Wider Wisdom," in *The Royal Priesthood: Essays Ecclesiological and Ecumenical* (Grand Rapids, MI: Eerdmans, 1994), 126.

Chapter Five

1. Kenda Creasy Dean, "Fessing Up: Owning Our Theological Commitments," in *Starting Right: Thinking Theologically about Youth Ministry*, eds. Kenda Creasy Dean, Chap Clark, and Dave Rahn (Grand Rapids, MI: Zondervan, 2001), 29.

2. Kenda Creasy Dean, *Practicing Passion: Youth and the Quest for a Passionate Church* (Grand Rapids: William B. Eerdmans Publishing Company, 2004), 62. Creasy Dean borrows the term "patchwork self" from David Elkind who develops the concept in *All Grown Up and No Place to Go* (Reading, MA: Addison-Wesley, 1998).

3. Marcus Borg, *Jesus: A New Vision: Spirit, Culture and the Life of Discipleship* (San Francisco, CA: Harper and Row, 1987), 79-93.

4. J. Richard Middleton and Brian J. Walsh, *Truth Is Stranger than It Used to Be: Biblical Faith in a Postmodern Age* (Downers Grove, IL: InterVarsity Press, 1995), 107.

5. The Mesopotamian myth, *Enuma Elish*, is a lengthy epic of which the Babylonian story of beginnings is a part. For more, see Stephanie Dalley, "The Epic of Creation," in *Myths from Mesopotamia: Creation, the Flood, Gilgamesh and Others* (Oxford, UK: University of Oxford Press, 1989), 228-277. Also see Middleton and Walsh, 108-42.

6. Jürgen Goetzmann, "*metánoia.*" *New International Dictionary of New Testament Theology*, vol. 1, ed. Colin Brown. (Grand Rapids, MI: Zondervan, 1986), 357.

7. Tom Sine, *Mustard Seed Versus McWorld: Reinventing Life and Faith for the Future* (Grand Rapids, MI: Baker Books, 1999), 23.

8. Fred Craddock, *Luke*. Interpretation: A Bible Commentary for Teaching and Preaching (Louisville, KY: John Knox Press, 1990), 164.

9. Richard Foster, *Celebration of Discipline: The Path to Spiritual Growth*, 3d ed. (San Francisco, CA: HarperSanFrancisco, 1998), 111.

10. Dallas Willard, *The Divine Conspiracy: Rediscovering Our Hidden Life in God* (San Francisco, CA: Harper Collins, 1998), 279.

11. The conversations initiated by BikeMovement continue at www.bikemovement.org.

12. Douglas John Hall, *The Cross in Our Context: Jesus and the Suffering World* (Minneapolis, MN: Fortress Press, 2003), 36-37.

13. Stanley Grenz, *Created for Community: Connecting Christian Belief with Christian Living*, 2d ed. (Grand Rapids: Baker Books, 1998), 207.

14. Zach Hunter, *Be the Change: Your Guide to Freeing Slaves and Changing the World* (Grand Rapids, MI: Zondervan, 2007).

15. Jürgen Moltmann, *The Crucified God* (Minneapolis, MN: Fortress Press, 1993), 19.

16. Creasy Dean, *Practicing Passion*, 159.

17. See Creasy Dean and Foster, *The Godbearing Life*, 185-93.

18. David F. White, *Practicing Discernment with Youth: A Transformative Youth Ministry Approach* (Cleveland, OH: The Pilgrim Press, 2005).

19. Advent Conspiracy, www.adventconspiracy.org, is a helpful resource.

Chapter Six

1. Howard A. Snyder, *Models of the Kingdom* (Nashville, TN: Abingdon Press, 1991), 147.

2. Bill Romanowski's book, *Eyes Wide Open: Looking for God in Popular Culture* (Baker Book House, 2001), is a helpful resource, as are the links on Gordon Matties' web page (See www.cmu.ca/faculty/gmatties/). Matties is professor of Theology at Canadian Mennonite University in Winnipeg, Manitoba.

3. Chap Clark, "The Changing Face of Adolescence: A Theological View of Adolescent Development," in *Starting Right: Thinking Theologically About Youth Ministry*, eds. Kenda Creasy Dean, Chap Clark, and Dave Rahn, 41-61 (Grand Rapids, MI: Zondervan, 2001), 50.

4. These ideas came from Chap Clark, *The Youth Worker's Handbook to Family Ministry: Strategies and Practical Ideas for Reaching Your Students' Families* (Grand Rapids, MI: Zondervan, 1997).

5. I am indebted to Marva J. Dawn, author of *Truly the Community: Romans 12 and How to Be the Church* (Grand Rapids, MI: Eerdmans, 1992), for this idea.

6. Marion Bontrager at Hesston College in Hesston, Kansas, requires a more advanced assignment called *Heilsgeschichte*, meaning "salvation history," in the college's Biblical Literature course.

7. For more information, see www.d-e-o.org.

8. In Doug Fields' discussion of communicating the process of the youth ministry's spiritual growth plan, you'll find a well organized, clearly guided program that can be accomplished with little involvement from the broader adult populace of the church. See Doug Fields, *Purpose Driven Youth Ministry: 9 Essential Foundations for Healthy Growth* (Grand Rapids, MI: Zondervan, 1998) 209-29.

Postlude

1. I am indebted to Eugene Peterson for this approach to ministry. Kenda Creasy Dean described youth ministry as the "Art of Faithful Improvisation." See *Practicing Passion: Youth and the Quest for a Passionate Church* (Grand Rapids, MI: William B. Eerdmans Publishing Company, 2004), 22-24.

Bibliography

Adolescence/Youth/Family

Arnett, Jeffrey Jenson, ed. *Readings on Adolescence and Emerging Adulthood.* Upper Saddle River, NJ: Prentice Hall, 2002.

Borgman, Dean. *Hear My Story: Understanding the Cries of Troubled Youth.* Peabody, MA: Hendrickson Publishers, 2003.

Clark, Chap. *Hurt: Inside the World of Today's Teenagers.* Grand Rapids, MI: Baker Academic, 2004.

Elkind, David. *The Hurried Child: Growing Up Too Fast Too Soon*, 3d ed. Cambridge, MA: Perseus Books, 2001.

_____. *Ties that Stress: The New Family Imbalance.* Cambridge, MA: Harvard University Press, 1994.

Hersch, Patricia. *A Tribe Apart: A Journey into the Heart of American Adolescents.* New York, NY: Ballantine Books, 1998.

Males, Mike A. *Framing Youth: 10 Myths about the Next Generation.* Monroe, ME: Common Courage Press, 1999.

Pipher, Mary. *Reviving Ophelia: Saving the Selves of Adolescent Girls.* New York, NY: Ballantine Books, 1994.

Powers, Ron. *Tom and Huck Don't Live Here Anymore: Childhood and Murder in the Heart of America.* New York, NY: St. Martin's Press, 2001.

Smith, Christian with Melinda Denton. *Soul Searching: The Religious and Spiritual Lives of American Teenagers.* New York, NY: Oxford University Press, 2005.

Church

Brownson, James, Inagrace T. Dietterich, Barry A. Harvey, and Charles C. West. *Stormfront: The Good News of God.* Grand Rapids, MI: William B. Eerdmans Publishing Company, 2003.

McLaren, Brian. *The Church on the Other Side: Doing Ministry in the Postmodern Matrix.* Grand Rapids, MI: Zondervan, 2000.

_____. *The Secret Message of Jesus: Uncovering the Truth that Could Change Everything.* Nashville, TN: W Publishing Group, 2006.

Sine, Tom. *Mustard Seed Versus McWorld: Reinventing Life and Faith for the Future.* Grand Rapids, MI: Baker Books, 1999.

Culture

Beaudoin, Tom. *Consuming Faith: Integrating Who We Are with What We Buy*. Lanham, MD: Sheed & Ward, 2007.

Budde, Michael L. *The (Magic) Kingdom of God*. Boulder, CO: Westview Press, 1997.

Clapp, Rodney, ed. *The Consuming Passion: Christianity and the Consumer Culture*. Downers Grove, IL: InterVarsity Press, 1998.

Hughes, Richard T. *Myths America Lives By*. Urbana, IL: University of Illinois Press, 2003.

Klein, Naomi. *No Logo: Taking Aim at the Brand Bullies*. New York, NY: Picado, 1999.

Middleton, J. Richard, and Brian J. Walsh. *Truth Is Stranger than It Used to Be: Biblical Faith in a Postmodern Age*. Downers Grove, IL: InterVarsity Press, 1995.

Miller, Vincent J. *Consuming Religion: Christian Faith and Practice in a Consumer Culture*. New York, NY: Continuum, 2003.

Rempel, Henry. *A High Price for Abundant Living: The Story of Capitalism*. Waterloo, ON: Herald Press, 2003.

Romanowski, William D. *Eyes Wide Open: Looking for God in Popular Culture*. Grand Rapids, MI: Baker Book House, 2001.

Rushkoff, Douglas. *Coercion: Why We Listen to What "They" Say*. New York, NY: Riverhead Books, 1999.

Sweet, Leonard. *SoulTsunami: Sink or Swim in New Millennium Culture*. Grand Rapids, MI: Zondervan, 1999.

Youth Ministry

Borgman, Dean. *When Kumbaya Is Not Enough: A Practical Theology for Youth Ministry*. Peabody, MA: Hendrickson, 1997.

Creasy Dean, Kenda. *Practicing Passion: Youth and the Quest for a Passionate Church*. Grand Rapids, MI: William B. Eerdmans Publishing Company, 2004.

Creasy Dean, Kenda, and Ron Foster. *The Godbearing Life: The Art of Soul Tending for Youth Ministry*. Nashville, TN: Upper Room Books, 1998.

Creasy Dean, Kenda, Chap Clark, and Dave Rahn, eds. *Starting Right: Thinking Theologically About Youth Ministry*. Grand Rapids, MI: Zondervan, 2001.

DeVries, Mark. *Family-Based Youth Ministry: Reaching the Been-There, Done-That Generation*. Downers Grove, IL: InterVarsity Press, 1994.

Duerksen, Carol. *Building Together: Developing Your Blueprint for Congregational Youth Ministry*. Scottdale, PA: Faith & Life Resources, 2001.

Hochstetler, Ritch. "Thirsty for the Reign: A Kingdom Theology for Youth Ministry, Part Two." *Direction* 31 (Fall 2002): 176-85.

Jones, Tony. *Postmodern Youth Ministry: Exploring Cultural Shift, Creating Holistic Connections, Cultivating Authentic Community*. Grand Rapids, MI: Zondervan, 2001.

Loewen, Wendell. "Thirsty for the Reign: A Kingdom Theology for Youth Ministry, Part One." *Direction 31* (Spring 2002): 35-45.

Robbins, Duffy. *This Way to Youth Ministry: An Introduction to the Adventure*. Grand Rapids, MI: Zondervan, 2004.

White, David. *Practicing Discernment with Youth: A Transformative Youth Ministry Approach*. Cleveland, OH: Pilgrim Press, 2005.

The author

DEL GRAY

Wendell J. Loewen has taught at Tabor College since 1997 in the areas of youth, church, and culture. A graduate of Mennonite Brethren Biblical Seminary (MDiv) and Fuller Theological Seminary (DMin), he speaks regularly at retreats, conferences, and training events. His writing has appeared in *Direction* and *Christian Leader*, and in Carol Duerksen's *Building Together: Developing Your Blueprint for Congregational Youth Ministry* (Faith & Life Resources, 2001). He lives in Hillsboro, Kansas, with his wife Shelly and three children.